T0291321

Excellence in Supply Chain Management

Recent decades have witnessed an explosion in supply chain complexity. Very few firms have succeeded in building excellent supply chains and employing supply chain management (SCM) as a competitive advantage. For the ones which have developed enhanced supply chain design and process capabilities, their performance has far exceeded their competitors'. While for the vast majority of firms, SCM still remains a means of reducing costs and improving efficiency, for the excellent ones, SCM has turned into a source for value creation. What factors drive firms towards supply chain excellence? How can real differentiation be created through supply chains? *Excellence in Supply Chain Management* examines the characteristics and features of firms that excel in SCM.

Balram Avittathur is a Professor of Operations Management at the prestigious Indian Institute of Management Calcutta (IIM Calcutta) at Kolkata, India, and has been there since 1999. He holds a Fellow of Management (PhD) from the Indian Institute of Management Bangalore (1999). He specializes in the broad area of supply chain management. His research interests also include applications of game theory in operations management and operations management for environmental sustainability.

Debabrata Ghosh is Associate Professor at the Malaysia Institute for Supply Chain Innovation (MISI). Prior to this, he was a faculty member at the Indian Institute of Management Calcutta, India. He holds a Fellow Programme in Management (PhD) from the Indian Institute of Management Bangalore. His research interests lie in the areas of supply chain issues in emerging economies, sustainable operations, and supply chain coordination.

Routledge Focus on Management and Society

Series Editor: Anindya Sen

Professor of Economics, Indian Institute of Management Calcutta, Kolkata, West Bengal, India

The invisible hand of market has today been replaced by the visible hand of managerial capitalism. As the power and role of the managers have expanded, the world also has become more dynamic and volatile. To run their organisations more efficiently, the managers need to be aware of new developments taking place all around them. The Focus series addresses this need by presenting a number of short volumes that deal with important managerial issues in the Indian context. Volumes in the series will cover topics not only of perennial interest to managers but also emerging areas of interest like neuro marketing. Some of the well-established areas of research like bottom-of-the-pyramid marketing will be dealt with specifically in the Indian context, as well as critical developments in other fields, like Auction Theory.

The series is designed to introduce management theorists and researchers (as well as the lay public) to a diverse set of topics relevant directly or peripherally to management in a concise format, without sacrificing basic rigour.

Neuromarketing in India
Understanding the Indian Consumer
Tanusree Dutta and Manas Kumar Mandal

Poor Marketing
Insights from Marketing to the Poor
Ramendra Singh

Strategic Change and Transformation
Managing Renewal in Organisations
Swarup K Dutta

Excellence in Supply Chain Management
Balram Avittathur and Debabrata Ghosh

For a full list of titles in this series, please visit: www.routledge.com/Routledge-Focus-on-Management-and-Society/book-series/RFMS

Excellence in Supply Chain Management

Balram Avittathur and Debabrata Ghosh

Routledge
Taylor & Francis Group

LONDON AND NEW YORK

First published 2020
by Routledge
2 Park Square, Milton Park, Abingdon, Oxon OX14 4RN

and by Routledge
52 Vanderbilt Avenue, New York, NY 10017

*Routledge is an imprint of the Taylor & Francis Group,
an informa business*

British Library Cataloguing-in-Publication Data
A catalogue record for this book is available from the British Library

Library of Congress Cataloging-in-Publication Data
A catalog record for this book has been requested

ISBN: 978-0-367-08589-6 (hbk)
ISBN: 978-0-429-02687-4 (ebk)

Typeset in Times New Roman
by Apex CoVantage, LLC

To
Prof. Janat Shah, Director – Indian Institute of Management Udaipur
Our doctoral advisor at IIM Bangalore

Sita, Arjun, my parents and teachers – BA
Floya, Arya, my parents and teachers – DG

Contents

Abbreviations

3PL	third-party logistics
AM	additive manufacturing
ATO	assembled to order
B2C	business-to-consumer
CPFR	Collaborative Planning Forecasting Replenishment
EOQ	economic order quantity
ERP	enterprise resource planning
GST	goods and services tax
IoT	Internet of Things
MAD	mean absolute deviation
MAPE	mean absolute percentage error
MRP	material requirement planning
MTO	made to order
MTS	made to stock
SCM	supply chain management
SKU	stock keeping unit
TPS	Toyota Production System
TTR	time to recovery
TTS	time to survive
VMI	vendor managed inventory
VUCA	volatile, uncertain, complex, and ambiguous
WTO	World Trade Organization

Preface

The silk trade that existed between China, India, and several nations of Asia and Europe for centuries is evidence of the existence of global supply chains from ancient times. The term *supply chain management* (SCM), however, formally originated in the 1980s, recognizing the fact that one firm cannot solely manage all the activities involved in procuring and converting raw materials into finished products and supplying the finished products to the end customers. Interest in SCM, both in practice and academia, has significantly grown as fascinating advances have taken place with the rise of information technology. Motivated by these advances, a few scholars in the 1990s and even in today's era have suggested that SCM would become an insignificant aspect of managing a firm owing to the progress information technology would make.

In the last two decades, however, while information technology has made great strides and communication technologies have progressed at a rapid pace, achieving excellence in SCM has remained a daunting challenge for many firms across the world. Large numbers of retailing firms continue to be burdened by the challenges of stockouts and clearance sales. Manufacturing firms struggle with demand forecasting errors and unmet monthly targets. The truth is that complexity in managing supply chains has grown manifold. Most firms, as a result, describe SCM as a very complex activity. However, a few firms have built excellent supply chains and credit SCM as the principal source of their competitive advantage. We hypothesize that while for the vast majority of firms, SCM is still only a means of reducing costs and improving efficiency, for the excellent ones, SCM is driven by customer centricity. These are firms which constantly work on ensuring that their efficiency and effectiveness goals are aligned with each other rather than being in conflict. *Excellence in Supply Chain Management* is our modest attempt to understand the characteristics and features of firms that excel in SCM.

While this book is written keeping in mind practicing managers in SCM and allied business functions as the readers, it has not ignored the readership that is less familiar with SCM. Through 11 chapters, we examine the various practices that have evolved in SCM and strategies that make supply chains win. Unlike a conventional textbook or manager's reference guide, this book attempts to push the reader to think about why things are happening the way they are and how they should be if a firm intends to strive towards SCM excellence.

Chapter 1 introduces the reader to operations management, SCM, and their evolution up to the present. The next two chapters, "Inventory Management" (Chapter 2) and "Forecasting and Demand Planning" (Chapter 3), describe the concepts that have a significant bearing on SCM. Chapter 4 explores the evolution of SCM, the role of intangible losses on supply chain performance, and SCM's role in developing a sustainable competitive edge.

Chapters 5 to 8 cover the various facets of SCM. In Chapter 5, which is on supply chain coordination, we examine the role of contracts and integration on improving coordination and reducing issues like the bullwhip effect. Chapter 6 examines various issues in procurement and vendor management, while Chapter 7 discusses the importance of supply chain risk management for SCM excellence. In Chapter 8, we look at various aspects of product and supply chain network design that have a great bearing on SCM excellence.

The last three chapters examine various supply chain issues that have assumed significance in recent years. While Chapter 9 examines the importance of being green and sustainability in SCM, Chapter 10 describes some basic analytics that any supply chain manager should be aware of. We conclude the book with the chapter on operations and supply chain management in the digital era (Chapter 11). This chapter, authored by Prasad Ramakrishnan and Axel Zeijen, experts with considerable industrial experience, examines the role played by digital disruption, cognitive technologies, artificial intelligence, and additive manufacturing, and concludes with a section on leadership amidst disruptive change. Widespread application of these innovations is going to have a significant impact on SCM, and SCM managers should have a deep understanding of them to be able to successfully navigate their field in the future.

Acknowledgements

Our sincere thanks to Prof. Anindya Sen for encouraging us to embark on the task of writing this book and for constantly supporting us at various stages.

1 Operations and supply chain management

The initial journey

The excellence displayed by Amazon, Apple, Dell, Walmart, and Zara, to name a few firms, in the past few decades has indeed made the topic of supply chain management (SCM) omnipresent in any discussion of the present-day functioning of firms. While many experts have attempted to present SCM as a new field in management, many others see it as progress made by the broad area of operations management. We would subscribe to the latter view and devote this chapter to a broad understanding of operations management and operations strategy.

Operations management defined

Operations management is a *crucial function in any organization and involves the design and control of processes through which inputs or raw materials are transformed into service outcomes or finished products as desired by the customers.* The transformation processes employ different resources, like land, labour, and capital. Capital includes various sorts of buildings, machinery, transport equipment, and technologies like computing hardware and software. Operations management transformation processes could be of different types. Conversion of crude oil into finished products like petrol and diesel by an oil refinery is an example of physical transformation. A passenger travelling from one city to another in an airline is an illustration of locational transformation.

While processes that transform raw materials to finished products could trace their history to early human civilization, an organized manner of managing operations is typically considered to be a by-product of the Industrial Revolution. John D. Rockefeller established the Standard Oil Company in 1870, and in a matter of a few years, the company controlled 90% of America's refining capacity. While focussing on economies of scale to reduce its costs, the firm also set up processes in place to ensure that its products had consistent quality.[2] In 1913, Henry Ford caught the attention of the world by setting up a moving assembly line at Ford Motor Company. This, along with labour specialization, enabled him to bring down the chassis assembly time from over 12 hours to just 1 hour and 33 minutes.[3]

The twin pillars of operations management

The assembly line revolution at Ford is typically regarded as the dawn of the mass production era. Mass production symbolized the pursuit of economies of scale with low variety as a means of offering products at a low price and making them accessible to a greater number of customers, which in turn would drive scale further. This meant the replacement of many small factories by a fewer number of large factories. In America, automobile production started concentrating in and around Detroit. In addition, Ford felt that offering cars in many colours would result in costly and time-consuming process changeovers, which in turn would reduce the utilization of the assembly line. He famously declared that Ford cars would be offered in any colour as long as it was black.[4] Along with economies of scale, firms started focussing heavily on maximum utilization of their resources as a means of spreading the overheads over a larger output and thus minimizing the unit cost of production. The field of industrial engineering, pioneered by stalwarts like Fredrick Taylor,[5] emerged in this background of firms pursuing **efficiency**, or the *most economical way of producing a good or delivering a service.*

Industrial engineering and its piece-wise solution to firm-level problems dominated much of the 20th century. Efficiency remained by far the main concern of operations management in the mass production era. Many concepts, mostly with the goal of minimizing cost or time – like aggregate production planning, inventory control, line balancing, material requirement planning, process analysis, scheduling, and statistical quality control – emerged during this period. The pursuit of efficiency did not necessarily translate into a high level of customer satisfaction. In fact, there were countless instances of efficiency pursuits resulting in customer unhappiness of some sort or other. An illustration of how an efficiency pursuit results in customer dissatisfaction is the case of deciding the optimal number of security counters at an airport based on average customer arrivals, which results in long queues when arrivals are more than usual. However, by the 1970s, change was looming on the horizon.

The twin oil shocks in the 1970s provided the opening for Japanese automakers like Toyota and Nissan to enter into the American market. Though the initial success was due to the fuel savings owing to their being smaller in size, the Japanese cars soon made an impact on the American customers because of their better quality and serviceability.[6] The American manufacturers were curious to understand the secrets of firms like Toyota in maintaining high-quality, low-inventory, and pull-based production. They discovered what Toyota referred to as the Toyota Production System (TPS), which eventually came to be known as lean production. Contrary to just enhancing efficiency as in mass production, lean production strived to enhance both efficiency and effectiveness. **Effectiveness** means an *organization doing the right things from the perspective of its customers, whether it is regarding quality, delivery, or variety.*

Until the arrival of TPS, it was widely felt that efficiency and effectiveness were at conflict with each other. After all, it was costlier to invest in processes that were of higher quality and operated on a pull basis. In the following decades, TPS inspired firms like Southwest Airlines, Dell Computers, and Walmart to develop their own models in operational excellence by pursuing the twin pillars of operations management – efficiency and effectiveness – simultaneously. Along with Toyota, these firms demonstrated that it was indeed possible to pursue gains in efficiency and effectiveness simultaneously if these objectives were considered at the design stage itself. For instance, Southwest Airlines has been a model of airline efficiency owing to quick turn-around times of its aircraft, while being a model of airline effectiveness (customer-centric) through a reputation built on punctuality, frequent service, low fares, and negligible baggage delays.[7]

Referring to Figure 1.1, a world-class firm[8] is superior to any other firm in its industry on both effectiveness and efficiency. The efficiency-effectiveness frontier (solid curve) represents the best-case efficiency-effectiveness combination at a given point in time based on the existing technologies and

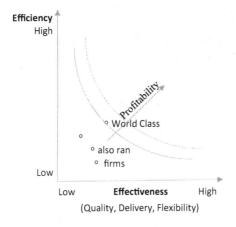

Figure 1.1 The efficiency–effectiveness frontier

management practices. However, through continuous improvement in both technology and management practices, it is possible to shift the frontier upwards (dotted curve).

Operations strategy: competing on operations

In 1969, Wickham Skinner argued that the "connection between manufacturing and corporate success is rarely seen as more than the achievement of high efficiency and low costs."[9] Over the years, various experts have argued about the need to go beyond just competing on efficiency. This paved the way for a field devoted to competing on operations, or simply operations strategy. Competing on operations implied that a firm could use one or more of the operations strategy elements, namely cost, quality, flexibility, and delivery. For over 40 years, Southwest Airlines has been the cost leader in the American domestic airline industry with its cost per available seat mile less than the industry by 25%.[10] As mentioned earlier, the airline follows a strategy of spending very little time on the ground so that its aircraft are in the air for as much time as possible. By focussing on the sales per square foot, Costco has emerged as one of the most efficient retailers in America.[11]

The inroads made into the American market for sophisticated products like automobiles and electronic products by Japanese firms like Toyota and Sony brought global attention to competing on quality. David Garvin argued that while a marketing view of higher quality is better performance, enhanced features, and other improvements that increase cost, the manufacturing view of better quality is conformance to specifications and "doing it right the first time," which helps reduction of cost.[12] While making the case for quality as an important element of strategy, he proposed eight dimensions of product quality, namely, performance, features, reliability, conformance, durability, serviceability, aesthetics, and perceived quality. Apple has been an example of a firm that has built a very strong brand based on the high quality that it offers in its products like mobile phones, personal computers, and tablets. As a result, it has been able to charge a handsome premium on its products and command a high customer loyalty.

By the 1980s, more and more firms had started migrating from low-variety mass production to high variety and customization (mass customization).[13] One of the examples of mass customization cited is that of National Bicycles of Japan, where a customer could choose a customized bicycle that could be from among a million variants possible. Offering higher variety and customization required a firm to be flexible in its operations. The flexibility could be on quickly changing over from one product type to another or in scaling up/down the production volume of a particular product or in introducing new products as required by the customers. While the argument till then was that being flexible would come at a high cost, firms like Toyota were able to demonstrate that it was possible to be efficient and flexible at the same time. While being an efficient car maker, Toyota was able to show that it could make changeovers from one model to another quickly as it positioned itself as a firm offering higher variety and greater customization than its competitors. In India, Asian Paints pioneered mass customization by delaying the product differentiation to the retail end. By installing colour dispensers at its retail outlets, Asian Paints has become very flexible with respect to meeting customer demand.

While quality caught the headlines in the 1970s and flexibility in the 1980s, the 1990s became the decade when firms realized the potential of competing on delivery. As the manufacturing world gradually shifted from mass production to lean production and from low variety to high variety and as business started getting more global, it became evident that delivery would be a new dimension for firms to impress their customers. With the advent of firms like Federal Express (subsequently known as FedEx), famous initially for its overnight deliveries, distribution of goods was no more the "dark continent of business," as described by the famous management guru Peter Drucker. FedEx and UPS were at the forefront in advancing technologies like GPS tracking and bar-coding, which enabled higher levels of automation in logistics activities. Subsequently, firms like Dell and Amazon pioneered the competition on delivery in their respective industries. Today, delivery is a broad concept that includes timely receipt of goods by the customer, in the correct quantity, and many other aspects of availability as per customer requirements.

For various reasons, it may not be possible for the same firm to be the best in its industry or peer group on all four elements of operations strategy. The focus on different elements of operations strategy should be aligned with other functional strategies as well as the overall organizational strategy. The term *world class firm* has been defined in different ways. Earlier, we described a firm as world class if it was on the efficiency-effectiveness frontier and ahead of its peers in both aspects. Similarly, a firm can be termed world class if it is able to be consistently ahead of its industry peers on all four operations strategy elements.[14] Toyota is a noteworthy example of a world class firm in the global automobile industry.[14] Another example of a world-class firm is Emirates Airlines. Launched in 1985, over three decades it has become a leading international airline, owing to competing well on all four elements of operations strategy. A fleet comprising many Airbus 380 aircraft and high utilization enable the airline to keep costs lower while focusing on high-quality in-flight and ground services, punctuality (delivery), and a worldwide network (variety, flexibility).[15]

Supply chain management (SCM)

With increasing globalization and competition no longer based on just cost or quality, the 1990s started seeing drastic changes in the way firms were organizing their supply chains. Higher cost and less flexibility of labour induced a lot of Western firms, particularly in America, to outsource many of the production activities that were happening in-house or from nearby localities to distant places like Mexico. With the fall in freight charges, owing to falling fuel prices and more efficient means of transportation, the manufacturing outsourcing started spreading to even more distant places like China. The Chinese government was also taking many steps to encourage manufacturing investment in their country. With a large skilled workforce available at very low wages, the landed cost in America of a product manufactured in China was lower than it would have been had it been manufactured in America itself, despite the higher transportation cost.

Simultaneously, great progress was happening on the information technology front. With the advent of the Internet, email, and enterprise software, distances were no longer a barrier to managerial decision making. The rise of firms like FedEx and UPS, as mentioned earlier, and technologies like bar-coding and GPS meant tracking of consignments could also be done online. More and more international cargo started moving through standard-size containers, and container ports started handling ships more quickly. The 1990s also witnessed the large-scale use of air as a mode of international logistics. This cut down lead times drastically and was a great help if the product was perishable or the demand was very difficult to predict. These changes in turn further accelerated the process of manufacturing outsourcing from the rich world to countries like China.

By the turn of the century, big multinational firms were more convinced than ever before that they did not have to be strongly present in the various aspects of the manufacturing value chain. It made greater business sense to outsource much of the manufacturing to lower-cost countries and be confined to higher-end activities like design and marketing. Apple symbolized this trend with manufacturing being totally outsourced to firms like Foxconn. With increasing levels of outsourcing, the supply chain challenge of such firms shifted from controlling the different internal functions to coordinating the various suppliers and logistics firms involved in the procurement, production, and distribution activities.

Supply chain management (SCM) has been defined in numerous ways. While developing a definition that is universal, it must be kept in mind that the SCM challenges vary widely from one industry to another and from one business model to another. The SCM challenges faced by the automobile industry are far different from the challenges faced by the apparel industry. The SCM challenges faced by Unilever, which is primarily a business-to-consumer (B2C) model are widely different from the challenges faced by GE Renewable Energy or Airbus, which are examples of the business-to-business (B2B) model. A theme common to the different SCM definitions is the *efficient and effective coordination of material and information flows among suppliers, manufacturers, distributors, and customers so that a wide variety of products could be delivered quickly while keeping costs as low as possible.*[16] While the supply chain of a product from raw material stage could pass through many tiers of suppliers, manufacturers, and distribution agents, we view the supply chain from the perspective of a firm and define a particular firm's supply chain as commencing from its suppliers and ending with where the product is acquired by its customers. Figure 1.2 is the pictorial description of the supply chain of a manufacturing firm (described as "manufacturer" in the diagram) in a B2C model.

SCM has evolved considerably in the last two decades. If the Dell fast assembled-to-order (customized) supply chain was the highlight of the early 2000s, the high variety and supply chain efficiency offered by Walmart caught the attention of the world in the remaining part of that decade. Apple, Amazon, and Zara are among different global firms that have dominated this decade with their fast and responsive supply chains. Despite the wide dissemination of aspects that contribute to supply chain management excellence in the last two decades, a large proportion of firms continue to see SCM as a major challenge and as an aspect that creates a strong competitive advantage. The following chapters deal with the various aspects critical to successful supply chain management. Through various examples, it also attempts to bring out the SCM characteristics that differentiate excellent SCM firms from the rest.

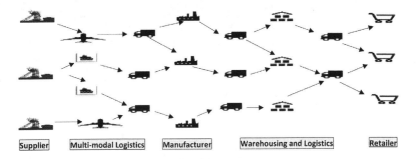

Figure 1.2 Supply chain of a B2C manufacturing firm

Strategic insights

- Excellent firms lead their industry peers on both efficiency and effectiveness. They invest continuously in technology and management innovations to shift the efficiency-effectiveness frontier upwards.
- Competing on operations is a characteristic of excellent firms, and they typically are industry leaders on operations strategy elements – namely cost, quality, flexibility, and delivery.

Notes

1 Simchi-Levi, D., & Fine, C. H. 2010. Your next supply chain. *MIT Sloan Management Review*, 51(2), 17–24.
2 Yergin, D. 1991. *The Prize: The Epic Quest for Oil, Money, and Power*. New York: Simon & Schuster.
3 Srinivasan, B. 2018. *Americana: A 400-year History of American Capitalism*. Penguin.
4 Duncan, J. 2008. *Any Colour, So Long as It's Black! Designing the Model T Ford, 1906–1908*. Auckland, NZ and Wollombi, NSW: Exisle Publishing.
5 Frederick, T. 1911. *The Principles of Scientific Management*. New York: Harper Bros.
6 *The Car Company in Front*. www.economist.com/special-report/2005/01/27/the-car-company-in-front
7 Gittell, J. H. 2003. *The Southwest Airlines Way: Using the Power of Relationships to Achieve High Performance*. New York: McGraw-Hill.
8 Wheelwright, S. C., & Hayes, R. H. 1985. Competing through manufacturing. *Harvard Business Review*, 63(1), 99–109.
9 Skinner, W. 1969. Manufacturing – Missing link in corporate strategy. *Harvard Business Review*, May–June 1969, 136–145.
10 Tully, S. 2015. *Southwest Bets Big on Business Travelers*. http://fortune.com/2015/09/23/southwest-airlines-business-travel/
11 *The Key Difference between Costco and Walmart*. www.forbes.com/sites/greatspeculations/2017/02/06/the-key-difference-between-costco-and-walmart/
12 Garvin, D. A. 1984. What does "product quality" really mean? *Sloan Management Review*, 25(1), 25–43.
13 Pine, B. J. 1993. *Mass Customization: The New Frontier in Business Competition*. Boston, MA: Harvard Business School Press.
14 Mahadevan, B. 2015. *Operations Management: Theory and Practice*. Pearson Education India.
15 Kumar, N., & Steenkamp, J. B. E. 2013. We are the champions. *Business Strategy Review*, 24(2), 52–58.
16 Shah, J., & Avittathur, B. 1999. Improving supply chain performance through postponement strategy. *Management Review*, 11(2), 5–13.

2   Inventory management

Managing inventory judiciously is a daily challenge for supply chain managers. Inadequate levels result in sales loss while excess levels result in locking of working capital or deterioration of the goods. Excess stocks may also force the seller to clear the inventory at a discount, owing to perishability or obsolescence reasons. The inventory level at a given point in time is a function of the different variations faced in the inward or outward movement of goods at the stocking point. Thus, a proper understanding of demand or supply uncertainties is crucial to good inventory management. Simultaneously, a supply chain manager should also ask the fundamental question of whether it is necessary to stock inventory at a particular point in the supply chain.

Role of inventory

Inventory serves multiple purposes in the management of a supply chain. *An important role of inventory is to balance the variations in demand and supply.* For instance, a firm pursuing high utilization of its production facility would typically plan to peg its capacity close to its average demand. However, as demand could vary across different time periods, owing to reasons like seasonality, the firm would build finished goods inventory when demand was less than capacity, while it would avail the material in finished goods inventory when demand was greater than capacity. The same argument is true with regard to holding raw material inventory, where arrival of raw material is volatile while its consumption is steady. This form of inventory could thus be described as a source of **capacity** in addition to other sources of capacities like regular time production, overtime production, or subcontracting.

As argued earlier, reducing costs through economies of scale started becoming a goal of firms with the advent of an organized manner of managing operations. These economies of scale were pursued not just in production but also while procuring raw material from suppliers or while transporting goods. For instance, a firm could save on ordering costs if material is ordered once a week instead of daily (see the following section on economies in ordering). Similarly, it could save on setup (changeover) cost and time if production batches were bigger. In transportation too, there were cost advantages in transporting through vehicles of larger capacity (say a truck with a 16-tonne payload capacity versus a truck with just a four-tonne payload capacity). The drawback, however, is that such economies would lead to carrying higher levels of inventory, which in turn would lock a higher level of working capital. The inventory generated because of ordering in batches is termed **cycle stock** inventory. For instance, if a household purchases sugar each time as a 5 kg package and if the consumption of the same is uniform, the cycle stock inventory on an average would be 2.5 kgs, as the inventory varies between 0 kgs and 5 kgs. Here, *inventory plays the role of facilitating economies in different supply chain activities like procurement, production, and transportation.*

Now, in the preceding example, let us argue that the household would like to carry a reserve of 2 kgs of sugar as a hedge against situations that happen without adequate notice, like the visit of guests at short notice, a temporary inability to do shopping, or a disruption to the routine due to bad weather. Then, the purchase would be made every time the sugar stock is down to about 2 kgs. This 2 kg reserve is described as **buffer** or **safety stock** inventory. *Acting as a buffer against uncertainties in demand or supply* is another important role of inventory.

It may be noted that we are making a distinction in the role inventory plays in balancing demand and supply variations from the role it plays as a buffer against uncertainties in demand and supply. While the former can be predicted rather accurately through past data (say Sunday sales are twice the weekday sales), we argue that the latter is difficult to predict accurately even with the availability of past data. In addition to these roles, inventory can also play other roles like a *hedge against price uncertainties* or *decoupling a stage in the supply chain against fluctuations in the previous stage* or in *making production scheduling more flexible.*

Inventory measurement

In the annual report of a firm, one can observe that inventory features in the balance sheet as an asset. It provides the aggregate value of various inventories held by the firm on the balance sheet date. Of course, more details are provided in the schedules of the balance sheet. However, the value of inventory as on a particular day of the year may not convey how well inventory is managed in the firm. Similarly, the cost of carrying inventory does not feature as one expense item in the profit and loss statement. The overall cost of carrying inventory comprises various subcomponents like (i) interest on capital held as inventory, (ii) rent or cost of maintaining warehouse facilities, (iii) cost of protecting and maintaining the inventory, and (iv) other fixed costs associated with maintaining inventory in the form of labour or capital, each falling under different expenditure heads in the profit and loss statement. In addition, notional losses like profit loss owing to inadequate inventory or possible higher returns on capital released because of lower inventory holding do not feature in the profit and loss statement. This makes the job of evaluating a firm's inventory management based on just the financial statements a challenging task.

For a better understanding of inventory movement, a monitoring that is as continuous as possible, say on a daily basis, is appropriate. Following are two examples of determining the daily closing stock, the first an instance of a retail point and the second an instance of a production plant. As the closing stock of a given day is the opening stock of the next day, only the inflow and outflow data of material is required except for on the first day. Once we have the closing (or opening) stock of all the days, we can determine the average closing (or opening) stock held at that inventory point. In addition, the variance in the stock held is another piece of information that could be of managerial significance.

Situation	Inventory at the end of a day (closing stock)
A retail point	Opening stock of the day + material received that day – sales that day
A production plant	Opening stock of the day + production that day – dispatches that day

The average inventory level so determined would still not convey how well the inventory is being managed. An inventory ratio like **inventory turnover** helps us understand the velocity of material movement more clearly. Inventory turnover at a given point in the supply chain tells us the number of times the inventory held there is sold or replaced in a year. For instance, if the value of a particular good sold annually by a retailer is $10,000 and if the value of this good held on an average at the retailer is $1,000, then the inventory turnover at the retailer of this good is 10.

$$Inventory\ turnover = \frac{Value\ of\ sales\ or\ outflow\ in\ the\ year}{Value\ of\ average\ inventory\ level}$$

As inventory turnover is expressed commonly in value terms, it allows aggregation over different goods transacted by the firm. In addition, inventory turnover enables us to easily fathom the inventory level held in number of days. In the preceding example, as the $10,000 sales is happening over a period of one year, or 365 days, we can argue that the inventory of $1,000 is equivalent to 36.5 days of sales. In other words, 365 divided by the inventory turnover tells us the average number of days the good is held as inventory at a given point in the supply chain.

Economies in ordering

As mentioned earlier, pursuing economies of scale in various supply chain activities is an important aspect of modern-day management. In 1913, Ford W. Harris proposed the famous economic order quantity (EOQ).[2] The model determines the optimal ordering quantity based on the trade-off between ordering cost and inventory carrying cost (see Figure 2.1). As the order quantity increases, the number of orders made and, hence, the ordering cost decreases, rapidly at a lower order quantity and slowly at a higher order quantity. At the same time, the inventory carrying cost increases in a linear fashion, as it is directly related to the order quantity. Hence, the total cost, which is the sum of ordering cost and inventory carrying cost, decreases till a particular order quantity and then increases from there on. This order quantity, where the total cost is minimal, is referred to as the EOQ. At the EOQ, the ordering cost is equal to the inventory carrying cost as can be seen from the figure.

The EOQ model makes assumptions, like constant ordering cost per order and inventory carrying cost per unit and constant and uniform demand. Though these assumptions are hardly true in real life, the model was considered an important milestone in operations management, specifically in inventory management. It became a popular topic for research, and many extensions of the original EOQ model were proposed by different scholars in this field. To the supply chain managers, the EOQ model conveyed the

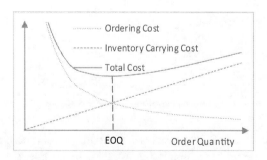

Figure 2.1 The economic order quantity

argument of an optimum in ordering; too low was inefficient from the viewpoint of ordering cost, and too high was inefficient from the viewpoint of inventory carrying cost. This idea of an optimum extended to many other activities like production and transportation overtime.

Service level and fill rate

Imagine a baker who has to decide the optimal daily starting inventory of a particular cake that she sells at $10 per unit. It costs her $8 to make each cake. Cakes left over at the end of the day are cleared at a discounted price of $5 per unit. The daily demand for this cake could be four, six, eight, or ten, with a likelihood of 20%, 25%, 30%, and 25%, respectively. What starting inventory should the baker opt for that maximizes her profit?

The preceding problem is one faced daily by innumerable supply chain managers in a variety of industries. A very low starting inventory may ensure that loss owing to leftovers is minimal, but it would also mean that a lower level of customer demand is met, which in turn could lower the profit that the firm could earn. Table 2.1 describes the calculations for different starting inventory levels for a given day.

The sales for a given demand and starting inventory will be the lower of the two values. The leftover for a given demand and starting inventory will be the starting inventory minus the sales.

Expected demand = sum of different demands weighted by their respective likelihoods

$$= 4 \times 0.2 + 6 \times 0.25 + 8 \times 0.3 + 10 \times 0.25 = 7.2$$

Expected sales = sum of sales at different demands weighted by respective likelihoods

$$= 4 \times 0.2 + 6 \times 0.25 + 6 \times 0.3 + 6 \times 0.25 = 5.6 \text{ for starting inventory of 6 units}$$

Expected leftover = sum of leftovers at different demands weighted by respective likelihoods

$$= 2 \times 0.2 + 0 \times 0.25 + 0 \times 0.3 + 0 \times 0.25 = 0.4 \text{ for starting inventory of 6 units}$$

Expected profit = expected sales times unit profit minus expected leftover times unit loss

$$= 5.6 \times (10 - 8) + 0.4 \times (8 - 5) = \$10 \text{ for starting inventory of 6 units}$$

Now let us try to understand service level and fill rate.

Table 2.1 Expected sales, expected leftover, expected profit, service level, and fill rate

Starting inventory	Sales for demand				Expected sales	Leftover for demand				Expected leftover	Expected profit ($)	Service level (%)	Fill rate (%)
	= 4	= 6	= 8	= 10		= 4	= 6	= 8	= 10				
4	4	4	4	4	4.00	0	0	0	0	0.00	8.00	20	55.56
5	4	5	5	5	4.80	1	0	0	0	0.20	9.00	20	66.67
6	4	6	6	6	5.60	2	0	0	0	0.40	10.00	45	77.78
7	4	6	7	7	6.15	3	1	0	0	0.85	9.75	45	85.42
8	4	6	8	8	6.70	4	2	0	0	1.30	9.50	75	93.06
9	4	6	8	9	6.95	5	3	1	0	2.05	7.75	75	96.53
10	4	6	8	10	7.20	6	4	2	0	2.80	6.00	100	100.00

Service level in the context of inventory management is defined *as the likelihood, typically expressed as a percentage, of a given inventory level meeting the demand fully*. As can be seen in the preceding calculations, for a starting inventory of six units, the demand is met fully only when it is four or six. As their likelihoods are 20% and 25%, respectively, the likelihood that demand is less than or equal to the starting inventory is 45%. Hence, we notice that the service level is 45% for a starting inventory of six units. The service level increases as the starting inventory increases. However, there is no increase in service levels for a starting inventory of five, seven, and nine, as can be seen in Figure 2.2. This is because the demands in this illustration are four, six, eight, and ten units, and a starting inventory of five, seven, or nine does not result in an increase in likelihood of demand being met fully compared to starting inventories of four, six, and eight, respectively. It is no coincidence that expected sales and expected leftovers increase with the starting inventory (Figure 2.2) and, hence, with respect to service level.

However, their rate of increase is not similar. In the preceding illustration, the expected sales increases faster for increases in starting inventory from four to eight, while the expected leftovers increases faster for an increase in starting inventory from eight to ten. Owing to expected sales increasing at a decreasing rate and expected leftovers increasing at an increasing rate, with respect to service level, it is not economically desirable to aim for an extremely high service level. In the preceding bakery illustration, the profit of the baker is highest ($10) when she decides to go for a starting inventory of six units with a service level of 45%.

Fill rate in the context of inventory management is defined *as the fraction or percentage of demand met for a given inventory or service level*. Referring to Table 2.1, it can be seen that fill rate can also be expressed as

Figure 2.2 Service level illustration

expected sales for a given inventory as a percentage of expected demand. While fill rate is a more precise measure of demand fulfilled than service level, it is often difficult to estimate, as actual demand is difficult to estimate in many situations. However, as the technological capabilities of firms increase with increased employment of data analytics tools along with online sales, it may be easier to track actual demand in coming years.

Basic inventory policies

An inventory policy for a stocking point refers to **when** and **how much** to order so as to minimize the total cost of ordering, inventory holding, and shortage. The order quantity or frequency is decided based on the trade-off between ordering cost and inventory carrying cost. The service level is decided based on the trade-off between safety stock inventory, carrying cost, and shortage cost. At the broadest level, there are two types of inventory policies – the continuous review policy and the periodic review policy.

In the continuous review policy, a fixed quantity is ordered every time the inventory position (inventory on hand + orders in pipeline) drops to the reorder point. The fixed quantity is typically determined based on the EOQ model, though other factors like supplier or transportation batch size may also determine the fixed quantity. For instance, the fixed quantity of gasoline ordered by a fuel station could be the capacity of the truck delivering gasoline. The reorder point is equal to the sum of (i) the expected demand during the normal time taken for replenishing the inventory (the expected lead time of replenishment) and (ii) safety stock to take care of surge in demand or delay in replenishment based on a target service level.

In the periodic review policy, the inventory position (inventory on hand + orders in pipeline) is reviewed at fixed intervals, and the quantity falling short of a predetermined level (order up to level) is ordered. The fixed interval, which for instance could be daily or weekly, is determined based on the trade-off between ordering/reviewing cost and inventory carrying cost. If T denotes the time between consecutive reviews and L denotes the replenishment lead time, then the order up to level is equal to the sum of (i) the expected demand during (T + L) time periods and (ii) safety stock for uncertainty in (T + L) time periods based on a target service level.

As can be seen from the description, both policies have their advantages and disadvantages. The continuous review policy suits situations where the replenishment quantity is fixed. The period review policy suits situations that permit ordering quantity to be variable and where it is difficult to review inventory on a continuous basis. However, with the advent of automation in inventory management, the latter is less of a challenge, and it is possible to foresee a future where continuous review policy would be more popular than periodic review policy. In reality, firms use variants of either policy to suit the operating conditions. It is also possible to use a hybrid policy that combines the features of both continuous and periodic review policies. An example of a hybrid policy is one where the review happens on a periodic basis, but the quantity ordered is an integer multiple of a quantity fixed in advance.

The single period inventory model

The single period inventory model has received immense attention in the field of supply chain management. It enables a manager to decide the optimal inventory to hold when faced with penalties or losses for overstocking as well as understocking. For instance, in the bakery inventory decision in the "Service Level and Fill Rate" section, the problem faced by the baker was to decide an optimal starting inventory given that overstocking would lead to unsold cakes while understocking would lead to an opportunity loss. Let us also imagine that the baker is not able to produce another batch of cakes on seeing a surge in demand. As unsold cakes must be cleared at the end of the day at a price less than cost, the baker faces a situation where both overstocking and understocking could lead to losses. This problem where (i) the inventory at the beginning of a period has utility only for that period, (ii) there is no scope for a subsequent order, and (iii) any leftover had to be salvaged at the end of the period is known as the single period inventory model. One of the best examples of a single period inventory model is that of the newspaper vendor who cannot sell the newspaper of a given day on the next day. In fact, the single period inventory model is also known popularly as the newsvendor problem, and the solution to the same was proposed in 1951 by Arrow, Harris, and Marshak.[3] Apart from inventory decisions of perishable or short-life cycle products, this model now has applications in many service situations like deciding the number of rooms or seats to be sold at different prices in a hotel or airline.

Let c_o and c_u denote the unit cost of overstocking and understocking, respectively. Then the optimal starting inventory will be a demand value that is at least equal to the fraction $c_u / (c_u + c_o)$ in the cumulative demand distribution. This fraction is known as the critical fractile. It could also be described in other words as the least demand value that is equal or greater to the service level equivalent to the critical fractile. Going back to the earlier baker illustration, it can be seen that c_o and c_u are equal to \$2 (= \$10 − \$8) and \$3 (= \$8 − \$5), respectively. The critical fractile is then equal to 2 / (2 + 3) = 0.4 or 40% service level. Referring to Table 2.1, it can be seen that a starting inventory of six units, which ensures a service level of 45% (the previous highest service level is 20%), is the demand value that ensures optimal profit for the baker.

Firms in the fashion industry are often accused of destroying unsold goods to maintain pricing power.[4] Given the quick obsolescence associated with the fashion products, the single period inventory model probably explains the understocking strategy (c_o could be greater than c_u if unsold goods are destroyed) that some of the fashion majors follow. Apart from maintaining pricing power, the shortage may help in creating an aura of exclusivity!

Strategic insights

- Instead of focussing only on the cost of working capital, excellent firms also factor in the indirect costs of inventory, particularly the ones that often get neglected as general overheads.
- Excellent firms take a strategic rather than a reactive view to inventory decisions. Firms like Toyota and Nestlé do not focus on utilizing capacity at very high levels; instead, they keep some part of their capacity to respond to peak demand so that peak sales need not be managed only from built-up inventory.
- Excellent firms constantly pioneer new technologies and practices to keep their batch sizes small. They also work constantly on managing supply and demand uncertainties better. All this enables them to operate with lower inventory and higher inventory turnover compared to their industry peers.
- As the service level increases, the expected sales increase at a decreasing rate while the expected leftover inventory increases at an increasing rate. Determining the optimal service level involves balancing the two, and reduction in inventory level (hence, inventory cost) should always be keeping its potential to reduce sales.

Notes

1 *Target Tests Retail 'Flow Center' for Faster, Nimbler Distribution.* www.wsj.com/articles/target-tests-retail-flow-center-for-faster-nimbler-distribution-1526299200
2 Harris, F. W. 1913. How many parts to make at once. *Factory, The Magazine of Management*, 10(2), 135–136, 152.
3 Arrow, K. J., Harris, T., & Marschak, J. 1951. Optimal inventory policy. *Econometrica: Journal of the Econometric Society*, 19(30), 250–272.
4 *How Fashion Industry Destroys Unsold Stock.*, www.scmp.com/lifestyle/fashion-beauty/article/2161123/luxury-fashions-waste-disposal-problem-chinas-part-it-and

3 Forecasting and demand planning

Forecasting and planning in a firm is a legacy of the era when utilization of resources was of paramount importance. In that era, commencing roughly from the mass production days of Ford Motors, the typical planning activities just before the start of the year were (i) forecasting demands at an aggregate level for different periods (say four quarters or 12 months) and (ii) aggregate capacity planning for these periods based on the forecasts. Then as the firm approached the respective quarter or month, detailed product-level forecasting and planning exercises would be carried out, and they would be the basis for various decisions on procurement, production, and distribution. The forecasting and planning activities are so crucial to the running of a modern firm that their importance led to a series of innovations, commencing with material requirement planning (MRP) in the 1960s and followed by others like enterprise resource planning (ERP) in the 1990s. Today, the emphasis is on forecasting and planning at a supply chain level whereby these exercises are no more limited to just within the firm. Increasingly, forecasts and plans are shared by firms located in a supply chain. However, despite these innovations and other progress made on the technological front, forecasting continues to challenge firms. Accurate forecasting still appears to be a dream for most firms to the extent that they are even exploring alternatives to the forecasting-and-planning-based production model.

Types of production systems

Before we discuss forecasting, it is important to know the different types of production systems. The two extremes of the production systems continuum are the made to stock (MTS) and made to order (MTO) production systems. An important objective of an MTS system is to operate at very high capacity utilization so that the cost of production is as low as possible. The sequence of activities, from forecasting to sales, is an outcome of designing a system to operate at high capacity utilization. However, high capacity utilization is not an important objective in an MTO system. In fact, MTO systems often operate with lot of slack, and the capacity is typically decided based on peak time demand. Production is taken up only after receipt of a firm order. Obviously, no demand forecasting is required in an MTO system. Table 3.1 compares the two systems on different details.

Owing to the emphasis on high-capacity utilization, a typical MTS system would have to carry inventory at different stages in the supply chain, resulting in inventory levels that are much higher than in an MTO system. The high inventory level also results in the supply chain lead time being high and supply chain velocity (speed of material movement along the chain) being slow. However, as MTO systems operate with sufficient slack, they tend to carry very low levels of inventory and, hence, have shorter lead times and higher supply chain velocity. However, on order lead time, the time taken to delivery from ordering time, an MTS system could be quicker than an MTO system, as the former typically transacts with the customer from a stocking point (say a retail outlet). In an MTO system, there could be a considerable time gap between ordering and receipt of the good. As the sales in an MTS system are from a stocking point, there is always considerable likelihood of the stock being much more or much less than demand. The former results in unsold goods that need to be disposed through a clearance sale, while the latter results in stock-outs that result in opportunity losses. As an MTO system produces based on actual orders, the likelihood of unsold goods is negligible. If there is sufficient slack in capacity, then the likelihood of opportunity losses owing to inability to take orders is also minimal.

Table 3.1 Comparison of MTS and MTO production systems

Detail	Made to stock (MTS) system	Made to order (MTO) system
Sequence of activities	Forecast ➡ Plan ➡ Produce/ distribute ➡ Stock ➡ Sell	Receive order ➡ Produce ➡ Dispatch
Demand forecasting	**Required**	**Not required**
Capacity utilization	High	Lower than in MTS
Inventory level	High	Low or nil
Order lead time	Nil	Few days to many months
Supply chain lead time	High	Lower than in MTS
Supply chain velocity	Slow	Fast
Clearance sales and stock-outs	High	Negligible
Customization and variety	Lower, lower variety	Higher, higher variety

Despite the various advantages in an MTO system, it is interesting to note that the production systems in various industries across the world are still dominated by MTS. Dell made a mark as a computer assembler by offering high customization to its customers. This was made possible by their following an assembled to order (ATO) system. In the past few decades, there has been a transition from pure MTS to a combination of MTS and MTO in different industries. Many automobile manufacturers today allow a much higher degree of customization than in previous years. While activities till the assembly line would still be operating on an MTS basis, these manufacturers would be operating the assembly line on an ATO basis. As described in Chapter 1, Asian Paints pioneered mass customization by delaying the product differentiation to the retail end. Here, too, the firm operates on an MTS basis till the retailer point and operates on an MTO basis at the retailer point.

Types of forecasting

Broadly, forecasting methods are of two types – qualitative methods and quantitative methods. Though it may appear that forecasting is foreseeing the future based on present or past data, it is not true that forecasting is only based on available data. Qualitative forecasting is employed primarily when there is an absence of data to carry out the forecasting exercise. A typical example of conducting a qualitative forecasting exercise is when a firm is launching a new product. Many qualitative forecasts are essentially based on judgements of experts or opinions of potential customers. Delphi Method and Market Survey are examples of qualitative forecasts. Quantitative forecasting is used as a mode of forecasting when sufficient data are available. Using past data, quantitative forecasting attempts to decipher patterns in demand and extrapolates the same to future time periods. There are various techniques in quantitative forecasting. We will dwell on two popular categories, namely causal forecasting and time series forecasting in the following sections.

Using data does not guarantee that the forecasts are error free. Owing to the considerable errors made in forecasts, forecasting is not considered an exact science. However, a lot of resources are devoted to this exercise, which adds to the costs of running a firm along with the costs to the firm as a result of inaccurate forecasts.

In 2001, Cisco, often considered an exemplar in high supply chain performance, announced that it would scrap approximately $2.5 billion worth of raw materials and posted a loss of $2.9 billion in a single quarter, resulting in a significant loss of market value for the firm.[2] While the company had advanced forecasting systems in place to predict demand and support planning, much of the recession that followed in 2001 was unanticipated and led to an inventory write-off worth billions. Several factors contributed to this incident. Much of Cisco's supply chain was outsourced, and lack of incentive alignment between supply chain partners led to a huge inventory pile-up in various parts of Cisco's supply chain. Additionally, the incident provided a reminder that forecasting systems can be unreliable.[3]

Causal forecasting

We often hear news reports mentioning increases in beer sales as the weather warms up, sales of electric vehicles increasing with increases in petrol prices, or home sales dampening with increases in interest rates. Demands for many products we consume are not constant or changing at a rate known in advance. Part of the variation in demand is explained by the variations happening to other things which have a bearing on the demand of such products. Causal forecasting helps a manager to understand linkages of demand with other variables. For instance, the average weekly sales of air conditioners for different weekly temperatures is as shown in Table 3.2.

In causal forecasting, the demand that we intend to forecast is regressed against the variables that influence that demand. Figure 3.1 describes a linear regression of average weekly air conditioner sales with weekly temperatures. The dotted line indicates an increasing trend in sales with weekly temperature.

While statistical software is ideal for a regression analysis, a causal forecasting exercise based on linear regression can easily be carried out in spreadsheet software, like Microsoft Excel. For the data in Table 3.2, one could arrive at a simple forecasting model as shown in the following by just using the intercept and slope functions in this software.

Average weekly sales (000s) = 825.75 + 55.27 × weekly temperature (in °C), where 825.75 is the intercept and 55.27 is the slope.

Table 3.2 Air conditioner sales data for different weekly temperatures

Weekly temperature (°C)	21	22	23	24	25	26	27	28	29	30
Average weekly sales (000s)	1825	2247	2559	1914	1733	2392	2303	2280	2524	2575

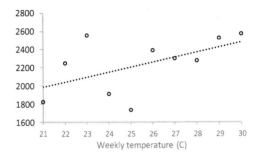

Figure 3.1 Causal forecasting illustration

Time series forecasting

The most common approach to data-based demand forecasting is using time series forecasting techniques. In time series forecasting, different patterns are deduced from chronologically arranged past demand data and used to predict the future demand. Some of the popular time series forecasting techniques are (i) moving average, (ii) weighted moving average, (iii) exponential smoothing, (iv) autoregressive moving average (ARMA), and (v) autoregressive integrated moving average (ARIMA). While readers with an interest in understanding these forecasting techniques in detail should refer to a book devoted to forecasting, we will dwell briefly on (i) moving average forecasting and (ii) exponential smoothing forecasting.

Past data comprise trend, business cycle, seasonal, and random components. According to Dervitsiotis,

> trend component refers to the long-term growth in average demand, business cycle component refers to deviation of demand from trend due to complex environmental influences, seasonal component refers to annual repetitive demand fluctuations and random component refers to the irregular residual in demand owing to many complex random forces.[4]

In Exhibit 3.1, we illustrate how demand could be decomposed to trend, seasonality, and random components to enable managers to forecast demand as accurately as possible.

Moving average forecasting

In an *n* period moving average forecasting, the forecast for a particular time period is the average of the demand observed in the previous *n* time periods. For instance, in a four-quarter moving average forecasting, the forecast for

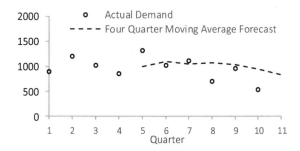

Figure 3.2 Moving average forecasting illustration

Quarter	1	2	3	4	5	6	7	8	9	10	11
Demand	897	1207	1023	859	1319	1032	1119	704	966	545	
Mov avg forecast					997	1102	1058	1082	1044	955	834

the fifth quarter is equal to the average of the demands observed in the first four quarters. The forecast for the sixth quarter is equal to the average of the demands observed in quarters two to five and so on for the remaining quarters.

Figure 3.2 describes a four-quarter moving average forecast for quarters five to 11 based on demand of quarters one to ten as shown in the grid.

The quarter five forecast is undertaken at the end of quarter four and so on. Referring to Figure 3.2, the forecast of 997 in quarter five is the average of the demands in quarters one to four, namely 897, 1207, 1023, and 859. The moving average forecast is essentially a smoothing of the demand with a n period lag. As n increases, the forecast gets smoother, though it may also result in loss of trend information inherent in the data.

Exponential smoothing forecasting

If F_t and F_{t-1} denote the forecasts for time periods t and t-1, respectively, and A_{t-1} denotes the actual demand in time period t-1, then in forecasting by simple exponential smoothing, the forecast for time period t is described as $F_t = F_{t-1} + k\left(A_{t-1} - F_{t-1}\right)$, where k is a smoothing constant that can take a value between 0 and 1.

Figure 3.3 describes an exponential smoothing forecast for k values of 0.3 and 0.7 for the demand data used in the moving average forecast example.

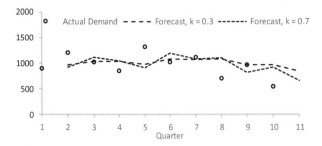

Figure 3.3 Exponential smoothing forecasting illustration

Quarter		1	2	3	4	5	6	7	8	9	10	11
Demand		897	1207	1023	859	1319	1032	1119	704	966	545	
Forecast for	$k = 0.3$		969	1040	1035	982	1083	1068	1083	969	968	841
	$k = 0.7$		928	1123	1053	917	1198	1082	1108	825	924	659

For quarter 1, we assume that there was an initial forecast of 1000. Using the preceding formula, the forecast for quarter two for $k = 0.3$,

$$F_2 = F_1 + k(A_1 - F_1) = 1000 + 0.3(897 - 1000) = 969.1 \approx 969$$

The lower the k value, the smoother is the forecast. In fact, for $k = 0$, the forecast would be same for all periods, while for $k = 1$, the forecast is equal to actual demand of the previous period.

Exhibit 3.1 Illustration of demand decomposition to estimate different components of demand

Managers involved in forecasting and planning need to understand the different components of demand as a first step in trying to forecast demand as closely as possible. Based on quarterly demand data of the past four years, from quarter three 2014 to quarter two 2018, the following table describes the decomposition of demand into different components, namely, trend, seasonality, and random.

After arranging the demand data in an ascending chronological order, the **first step** is to separate the seasonality component. For this goal, we first determine the moving average based on the number of

Year	Quarter	Demand	FQMA	CMA	DCMA	Seasonality	Qtr no	Trend	S x T	Residual
2014	3	822				1.080	1	704.2	760.5	1.081
	4	726	780.0			0.930	2	731.2	680.0	1.068
2015	1	648	764.0	772.0	0.839	0.812	3	758.3	615.7	1.052
	2	924	733.0	748.5	1.234	1.178	4	785.3	925.1	0.999
	3	758	744.5	738.8	1.026	1.080	5	812.4	877.3	0.864
	4	602	773.5	759.0	0.793	0.930	6	839.4	780.6	0.771
2016	1	694	854.0	813.8	0.853	0.812	7	866.4	703.5	0.986
	2	1040	964.0	909.0	1.144	1.178	8	893.5	1052.5	0.988
	3	1080	981.0	972.5	1.111	1.080	9	920.5	994.2	1.086
	4	1042	1018.0	999.5	1.043	0.930	10	947.6	881.2	1.182
2017	1	762	1034.5	1026.3	0.743	0.812	11	974.6	791.4	0.963
	2	1188	1026.0	1030.3	1.153	1.178	12	1001.6	1179.9	1.007
	3	1146	1057.5	1041.8	1.100	1.080	13	1028.7	1111.0	1.032
	4	1008	1056.5	1057.0	0.954	0.930	14	1055.7	981.8	1.027
2018	1	888				0.812	15	1082.8	879.2	1.010
	2	1184				1.178	16	1109.8	1307.3	0.906

Quarter	Average (D ÷ CMA)	Seasonality
Qtr 1	0.812	0.812
Qtr 2	1.177	1.178
Qtr 3	1.079	1.080
Qtr 4	0.930	0.930
Total	3.997	4.000

Trend	
Intercept	677.15
Slope	27.04

Legend:
FQMA: four quarter moving average
CMA: centred moving average
D ÷ CMA: demand ÷ CMA
S × T: seasonality × trend
Residual = demand ÷ (S × T)

seasons. In preceding data, the year has four quarters. So, if we wish to understand the seasonality owing to the quarters, then we use a four-quarter moving average (FQMA). If we are studying the month season effect in a year, then a 12-month moving average is used. If we are studying the day season effect in a week, then a seven-day moving average is used. Obviously, the data should be in the time unit that we are analyzing (month for month effect, day for day effect, and so on). When the number of periods in the moving average calculation is an even number, the moving average cannot be assigned to a period. The FQMA of quarter three 2014 to quarter two 2015, which is 780.0, falls between quarter four 2014 and quarter one 2015. In such instances the moving average has to be centred. Thus, the CMA for quarter one 2015, which is 772.0, is obtained by averaging 780.0 (FQMA for quarter three 2014 to quarter two 2015) and 764.0 (FQMA for quarter four 2014 to quarter three 2015). Next, the demand is divided by the CMA (D ÷ CMA). The average (D ÷ CMA) is then obtained for each season (refer to the smaller table). For quarter one, the value of 0.812 is the average of 0.839, 0.853, and 0.743. Often, the sum of the average (D ÷ CMA) for the different seasons will not add up to the number of seasons. In preceding illustration, the sum adds to 3.997, though the number of seasons is four. Hence, we need to proportionately adjust the average (D ÷ CMA) such that the sum equals four. The adjusted numbers represent the seasonality value of each season. For the preceding data, the peak season is quarter two with a seasonality of 1.178, and the leanest season is quarter one with a seasonality of 0.812. The column titled "Seasonality" indicates the values for the different time periods based on the seasonality values of the respective time periods.

The **second step** is to separate the trend component, which could be linear or non-linear. We assume a linear trend in the preceding illustration. The column titled "Qtr No" assigns integer values to each period in an increasing order with respect to time (1 for quarter three 2014 and so on). For a linear trend assumption, we linearly regress the demand data against Qtr No. This involves determining the intercept and slope such that the linear expression "Intercept + Slope × Qtr No" fits the past demand as best as possible. The intercept and slope for linear regression can be easily determined using spreadsheet software like Microsoft Excel. For the illustration here, the intercept and slope values are 677.15 and 27.04, respectively. Accordingly, the trend value for quarter four 2015, which is the sixth quarter in the past demand data, is 677.15 + 27.04 × 6 = 839.4. The column titled

"Trend" indicates the values for the different time periods based on the trend values of the respective time periods. It can be noticed that the trend changes by 27.04 as we move from one quarter to its neighbouring quarter.

The **third step** is to separate the residual component, which is left over after removal of seasonality and trend components. Assuming the past demand to be a product of seasonality, trend, and residual components, the residual can easily be defined as demand divided by product of seasonality and trend. In many instances, the residual component could be argued as the unexplained component of demand and be termed as a random component. In this illustration, the seasonality and trend together explain 760.5 (i.e., 1.080 × 704.2) of the 822 demand in quarter three 2014. The remaining 61.5 or 8.1% of 760.5 is the random component. The term *random* implies that though it is possible to estimate the extent of randomness for a given demand data set, it is not possible to predict the randomness for a given time period in advance. Analyzing the residual data in this illustration, one can notice that the expected value of the residual is unity, while the standard deviation is 0.096 or 9.6% of the expected value of the residual.

While illustrating a demand data set that is assumed to have only seasonality, trend, and random components, it is brought to the reader's notice that the demand data could also contain other components. One such component is business cyclicity, which is observed in the situation where the demand is observed to vary with business cycles. In such situations, it would be wrong to interpret that the residual component represents only randomness. For instance, by carrying out a three-period moving average of the residual data, it would be possible to determine the business cycle component. If this component is significant, then the random component will be equal to the residual divided by the business cycle.

Returning to our illustration, we now come to the question of forecasting demand for a future period. As expected, randomness is unity; the expected demand in a future period is equal to the product of seasonality and trend of that time period when we assume that the data comprise only seasonality, trend, and random components (product of seasonality, trend, and business cyclicity in the case where the business cycle component is significant). Thus, the expected demand in quarter three 2018 will be 1.080 times 1136.8 or 1228.

(Adapted from Dervitsiotis, Kostas N. 1981. *Operations management.* McGraw-Hill Companies)

Measuring forecast accuracy

As mentioned earlier, forecasting is often associated with considerable forecasting errors. The forecasting error is the absolute deviation of actual demand from the forecasted demand expressed as a percentage of forecasted demand. The forecasting error increases with the granularity of demand forecasted. For instance, the error associated with the demand forecasting of Apple iPhone X mobile phones in the London Metropolitan Area in the 20th week of the year will be higher than the error associated with demand forecasting of Apple iPhone mobile phones in the United Kingdom for the whole year. The former is a case where the demand is disaggregated on the product (a model vis-à-vis product line), geography (a city vis-à-vis a whole country), and time (one week vis-à-vis the entire year) dimensions. Two measures to judge the forecast accuracy, mean absolute deviation (MAD) and mean absolute percentage error (MAPE), are defined in the following. Absolute value is the magnitude of the measurement (deviation or percentage error) without regard to its sign (positive or negative). The notations A_t and F_t denote the actual and forecasted demands for time period t, respectively, and n denotes the number of time periods for which the forecast accuracy is being measured. The measures are numerically illustrated in Table 3.3.

$$MAD = \frac{\sum_{t=1}^{n} \left| A_t - F_t \right|}{n} \qquad MAPE = \frac{\sum_{t=1}^{n} \left| \dfrac{A_t - F_t}{A_t} \right| \times 100}{n}$$

Table 3.3 Numerical illustration of MAD and MAPE

Period	1	2	3	4	5	6	Sum	Mean
Actual demand, A_t	1319	1032	1119	704	966	545		
Forecasted demand, F_t	997	1102	1058	1082	1044	955		
Absolute deviation, $\left| A_t - F_t \right|$	322	70	61	378	78	410	1319	219.8 ← MAD
$\left| \dfrac{A_t - F_t}{A_t} \right| \times 100$	24.4	6.8	5.5	53.7	8.1	75.2	173.6	28.9% ← MAPE

Importance of short lead times

One of the demand components described in Exhibit 3.1 is randomness, which signifies that the same cannot be predicted in advance for individual time periods. As trend and seasonality components of demand are determined by a structured procedure, one could argue that the randomness component decides how accurate the forecasting is: the lower the randomness, the higher the forecast accuracy. While randomness for individual time periods cannot be predicted in advance, it is possible to estimate its expected level. It should also be noted that while forecasting demand, recent past data bear a greater influence than distant past data. The more recent data we have, the better would be the estimation of demand components like seasonality and trend. In other words, the weaker estimation of remaining demand components owing to not having sufficient recent past data naturally contributes to a higher level of randomness and, hence, greater forecast errors.

This brings us to the question of how early the forecasting is being done. If the forecasting horizon is the time between when the forecasting is done and when the actual demand is observed, then forecasting earlier implies a longer forecasting horizon. By an earlier argument, the longer the forecasting horizon, the greater the random component, and, hence, the higher the forecasting errors would be. What makes a firm forecast demand with a long forecasting horizon? The answer lies typically in the length of the supply chain. The longer the supply chain lead time owing to supplier constraints or the supplier being located far away or due to many stages in the supply chain, the longer will be the forecasting horizon. Thus, it is imperative in achieving high accuracy in forecasting for the firm to operate with short lead times.

The growing Indian automotive industry presents a fairly unique challenge to automakers in the country. Most of the passenger vehicles in India are delivered under the build-to-stock (BTS) strategy, while the build-to-order strategy (BTO) is primarily reserved for group orders of commercial vehicles. The passenger vehicle market has the presence of a large number of variants which are mostly sold through dealerships spread across the country. Despite the BTS model, where consumers can pick up any variant from the dealers the same day, interestingly, consumers in India tend to prefer particular brands and variants and are often ready to wait for a long period of time to receive those. This presents a unique challenge in forecasting and inventory management, since preference for particular variants often creates difficulties in planning, production, and stocking of finished vehicles, leading to long lead times. Further, sales of vehicles are also often influenced by festive seasons in India, making forecasting, capacity planning, and inventory management difficult. Long lead times for certain variants coupled with demand supply mismatch owing to inaccurate forecasts often leads to large inventories in supply chains.[5] This sometimes forces automakers to resort to temporary plant shutdowns to adjust for unsold inventories in their supply chains as happened in the case of Tata Motors, Fiat, and Maruti,[6] among others.

Product variety and forecast accuracy

Increased competition in recent times has encouraged firms to offer greater choice to the customer through higher product variety. Offering higher variety is widely seen as a means of boosting sales. A typical example is that of offering ice cream in many variants other than the simple vanilla flavour. What is the effect of higher product variety on forecast accuracy? As variety increases, the uncertain part of demand (randomness) for the individual stock keeping unit (SKU), explained in the previous section as the demand residual after separating the components like trend and seasonality, increases. As a numerical illustration, say a product is offered in just one variant only and has a sale of 100 units per day with a random variation of ±10 units (10% of the demand). The firm selling this product decides to introduce another variant to increase overall sales. The introduction of the new variant helps the firm to increase its aggregate sales by 20% to 120 units per day with a random variation of ±12 units. The question is what the random variation in demand for the two variants would be. If the new aggregate daily demand of 120 units comprises 80 units per day from the original variant and 40 units per day from the new variant, the greater flexibility to try a different variant at each purchase occasion results in the SKU random variation, expressed as a percentage of their demand, to be higher than the aggregate sales variation of 10%. The SKUs often turn substitutes of each other with relative demand fluctuation higher than what is noticed at the aggregate level. A variation of ±10 units (12.5% of the original variant demand of 80) and ±8 units (20% of the new variant demand of 40) is thus plausible in the preceding illustration. Increase in product variety contributes to greater randomness in demand for individual SKUs, and the random variation is typically higher for SKUs with lower demand than that of SKUs with higher demand. This explains why faster-moving SKUs generally exhibit lower relative variability in demand than their slower moving counterparts.

Reducing reliance on technique-based forecasting

The realization that forecasting is fraught with errors has convinced firms over time to search for alternatives to technique-based forecasting, particularly when the uncertainty in demand is high. Some firms, for instance Zara,[7] source from nearby suppliers so that procurement lead time is short. Asian Paints pioneered delayed differentiation of paint shades by postponing the mixing of pigments to the base colour to the retailer points.[8] This ensures that the firm does not have to do forecasting of individual colours and can instead focus on aggregate demand forecasting, which is far more accurate. Walmart pioneered collaborative forecasting and replenishment in 1996 to share its demand forecast with Warner-Lambert Co., supplier of Listerine.[9] Eventually, the software came to be known as Collaborative Planning Forecasting Replenishment (CPFR). It enabled suppliers to track online retail sales of items they supplied and synchronize their production accordingly. This spared suppliers the task of demand forecasting. Instead of forecasting demand, some retailers have shifted to quickly replenishing based on actual sales, whereby the order placed to the supplier at the end of the day is essentially the sales of that item on that day.

Rather than depending on technique-based forecasting at the SKU level, Levi's invested in a demand replenishment system so that orders reach the factory instantaneously, replenishments happen quickly from factories, and executives can track shipments real-time.[10] This quick replenishment strategy vastly reduced supply lead times. Increasingly, retailers and manufacturers are shifting the sales of their slower-moving SKUs from physical stores to online mode. Advance SKU forecasting becomes redundant if the firm can carry out the production and distribution activities within the delivery time promised. For instance, one of the goals of the Dell Direct MTO business model, which allowed customers to order their desired computer configuration online, was to eliminate costly and error-prone SKU-level forecasting.

Other illustrations of reducing reliance on technique-based forecasting include (i) offering only a portion of the total product line at a given time, (ii) designing and offering SKUs such that they complement sales, and (iii) phasing out SKUs that have passed their peak and are now slow moving. By offering only a portion of the total product line, for instance only 50 of 150 SKUs at a given point in time (say a month), the firm reduces its forecasting effort to just a third. While moving to the next month, some of the 50 SKUs would be taken out while an equivalent number from the remaining 100 SKUs would be added. Offering only a portion of the firm's product line helps in improving the forecast accuracy owing to higher sales per SKU. Such an initiative could also create an impression on the firm's consumers that its product line is very dynamic, which for products like apparel and toys could even contribute to a demand boost. Designing and offering SKUs such that they complement sales implies that certain combinations of SKU offering are more effective in controlling lost sales. For instance, a shortage of 5 kg detergent packs may push a consumer to buy 1 kg packs. However, the reverse may not be true. Hence, the forecasting could be at the detergent level (instead of SKU level, which would reduce the forecasting effort and inaccuracies), and the firm may overstock 1 kg packs while understocking 5 kg packs. Phasing out SKUs whose sales have been declining and have clearly become slow moving is another way of reducing the forecasting effort and improving accuracy.

Strategic insights

- Forecasting is not an exact science. Accuracy of forecasting depends on the inherent randomness in demand – the higher the randomness, the lower the forecasting accuracy. The randomness in demand in turn is a function of when the forecast is made – the earlier the forecasting, the higher the randomness. Hence, short lead times and forecasting horizons are extremely critical to achieving accurate forecasts.
- An MTS system operating at high capacity utilization experiences long lead times, which forces it to make demand forecasts well in advance. The longer the forecast horizon, the greater the forecast errors. Thus, there is a trade-off between the perceived efficiency gain from high capacity utilization and the losses owing to inaccurate forecasts.
- Excellent firms focus on building fast supply chains with short lead times that enable them to either do away with forecasting or minimize their reliance on it.
- Managing higher SKU variety comes with a trade-off between increased sales and increased errors in forecasting. It is very important to factor in this trade-off while launching new SKUs.
- Differentiating the fast- and slow-moving SKUs on the supply chain network employed (refer to Chapter 8 for details) is a characteristic of excellent firms.

Notes

1 Berinato, S. 2001. *What Went Wrong at Cisco in 2001?* www.cio.com/article/2441400/what-went-wrong-at-cisco-in-2001.html
2 Narayanan, V. G., & Raman, A. 2004. Aligning incentives in supply chains. *Harvard Business Review*, 82(11), 94–102.
3 Berinato, S. 2001. *What Went Wrong at Cisco in 2001?* www.cio.com/article/2441400/what-went-wrong-at-cisco-in-2001.html

4 Dervitsiotis, K. N. 1981. *Operations Management*. McGraw-Hill Companies.
5 Chandra, S., Ghosh, D., & Srivastava, S. K. 2016. Outbound logistics management practices in the automotive industry: An emerging economy perspective. *Decision*, 43(2), 145–165.
6 *Fiat, Tata Motors, Maruti May Shut Down Plants Temporarily*. www.hindustan times.com/autos/fiat-tata-motors-maruti-may-shut-down-plants-temporarily/story-mgUs7yBfGjU4njcVzs0ziJ.html
7 *The Management Style of Amancio Ortega*. www.economist.com/business/2016/12/17/the-management-style-of-amancio-ortega
8 Shah, J. 2009. *Supply Chain Management: Text and Cases*. Pearson Education India.
9 Verity, J. W. 1996. *Clearing the Cobwebs from the Stockroom*. https://web.archive.org/web/20121018090953/; www.businessweek.com/1996/43/b3498166.htm
10 Girard, K. 2003. *Supply Chain Partnerships: How Levi's Got its Jeans into Walmart*. www.cio.com/article/2439956

4 Supply chain management as a competitive advantage

In Chapter 1, we discussed what supply chain management (SCM) is and the factors contributing to its importance. In this chapter, we explore the progress of SCM over the decades as a tool enabling firms to compete. In the 1990s and even in the early 2000s, SCM was looked at as a means of building an efficiency or low-cost competence. However, in the past decade or so, it has been noticed that an "efficiency-only" focus contributes to the fragility of supply chains instead of building competence. The focus in recent times for many firms is increasingly on building responsive, agile, or resilient supply chains in order to pursue a sustainable competitive advantage.

Efficient supply chains

When Deng Xiaoping became the leader of China in 1978, no one could anticipate the events that were to follow, which would shape not just his country's role in the world economy but also the state of supply chains and SCM. Under his leadership, one of the early decisions was to reform the Chinese economy that had grown insular under Chairman Mao. In 1980, a special economic zone (SEZ) was set up in the small town of Shenzhen, close to the border with Hong Kong. Though the investments in the 1980s were mainly from the Chinese diaspora, China started catching attention for its huge availability of skilled labour at very low wages. At the same time, manufacturing firms in the Western world were facing a different challenge of high wages, a shortage of skilled labour, and strong labour unions. Two important economies, the United States of America and the United Kingdom, under Ronald Reagan[3] and Margaret Thatcher,[4] respectively, embarked on a course of free-market liberalization, which contributed eventually to the share of manufacturing in GDP as well as the workforce decline. In 2001, China joined the World Trade Organization (WTO) and signalled that foreign companies offshoring to China would be protected by international law and standard business practices. While this increased China's attractiveness as a manufacturing location, the Chinese leadership looked at foreign investment as a means of economic growth and access to various technologies.[5] Apart from the creation of the WTO, the 1990s also witnessed the wider acceptance of containerization, container terminals, integrated freight companies like FedEx and UPS in global logistics, and their use of efficient aircraft solely for the transportation of cargo.

By the turn of the millennium, the impact of these changes was visible at least in America. Walmart consolidated its position as America's biggest retailer. An economist, Emek Basker, while studying the causes and consequences of Walmart's growth,[6] attributes its rapid growth to its pursuit of huge supply chain efficiencies. Apart from investment in technology, he points to the focus on economies of scale in all aspects of its supply chain and the disproportionate share of foreign (Chinese) suppliers contributing significantly to its supply chain efficiency. For many years, Walmart purchases alone accounted for more than 10% of the Chinese goods imported into the USA. With its dominant position, Walmart ensured that it had significant bargaining power in its negotiations with suppliers and labour. The efficient supply chain was characterized by huge cost reductions through (i) high utilization of capacity; (ii) economies of scale and scope in ordering, procuring, manufacturing, logistics, and retailing; (iii) outsourcing and offshoring of various activities; and (iv) bargaining power vis-à-vis suppliers and labour.

India too observed globalization effects and increasing focus on supply chain efficiencies. Maruti Suzuki, India's leading car manufacturer, is a typical example of a manufacturer pursuing efficiency strongly so as to produce cars at the lowest cost. One of its efficiency initiatives with its vendors went by the tag "One Component One Gram." The goal of this initiative was to reduce the weight of each component going into the car by one gram.[7]

The changing supply chain landscape

With the collapse of the Soviet Union and the Cold War, the economic order started shifting towards the opening of economies. In India, the foreign exchange crisis in 1991 triggered the liberalization of its economy from many government controls. Across the world, tariffs and trade restrictions started easing. With the commencement of the WTO in early 1995, globalization kicked in with real force. As described in an earlier section, the initial emphasis of globalization appeared to be to exploit cost savings arising out of moving production and activities to lower-cost countries.

As the extent of globalization spread, many other changes started emerging. The reduction in costs translated into reduction in prices, which opened new markets and new customers for a wide variety of products. For instance, the automobile was no longer a luxury item in the developing world by the turn of the millennium. Many multinational majors like Nike and Pepsi were now having a strong presence in the developing world too.

Increased globalization also meant increased competition for a wide variety of products. After the initial phase of price reduction as the response to higher competition, the world started observing an increase in product variety as another response. In a wide range of industries, starting from food and apparel, the focus started to shift towards offering greater product variety. This increased sales and at times even market share.

The increase in product variety was soon followed by changing product life cycles. This phase was marked by the phenomenon of launching products with improved features at regular intervals. If one were to look at the example of the television set, a new model would be launched every year; a model launched in a particular year would see some improvements in its features compared to the model launched the previous year. If the television set launched in 2005 had a 24-inch screen with 80 channels, the one launched in 2006 would have a 28-inch screen with 100 channels. The industry clock speed, a measure of the new product introduction rate, started increasing in many product categories, including ones that were in the decline stage. Whether it was salt, ketchup, biscuits, or pens, firms were doing their best to make their products look as innovative as possible. In other words, changing styles, patterns, and designs were no more limited to just luxury product categories but became prevalent in everyday consumables.

The increase in clock speed and frequent new launches also meant that increased product variety was becoming too difficult to manage and often confusing for the customers. For instance, the Indian subsidiary of Unilever had bloated to around 110 brands by 2000. This was subsequently reduced to 30 power brands as part of a product rationalization exercise.[8] Thus, many firms in different industries started phasing out existing SKUs when new ones were getting launched. For instance, Apple discontinued sales of iPhone 6 when iPhone 7 was launched. As a result, product life cycle reduced significantly in many industries.

While observing the supply chain landscape in 2018, it is difficult to miss the high variety, fast clock speed, and short life cycle characteristics visible in many industries. While one may extol the virtues of higher customization and quicker churning of products in an increasingly customer-centric business world, it is also not possible to overlook the increasing levels of demand uncertainty and forecasting errors experienced by firms.

Drawbacks of an "efficiency only" supply chain

Though it is difficult to estimate the proportion of firms that view SCM only from the perspective of improving efficiency, a perusal of various reports available on the Internet and in other public domains indicates that efficiency is indeed still the primary SCM objective for many firms. In this section, we look at the drawbacks of each of the efficiency drivers described in the previous section on a firm's ability to manage demand.

High utilization of plant and machinery continues to be an important goal in various industries. The underlying argument here is that the fixed costs (say depreciation expense) associated with the capital resource would be spread across a larger production volume, helping the firm to reduce the unit cost of manufacturing.

For a given demand, as capacity utilization increases, the capacity cost declines. However, just as a bank ATM draws a long queue at peak load, a machine operating at high utilization would not be able to immediately process an order that it has received. By applying queuing theory concepts, it can be observed that for a supply chain operating at high utilization (high efficiency), the overall supply chain lead time increases exponentially at high capacity utilization levels (refer Figure 4.1). Similarly, the overall inventory level in the supply chain would also increase with capacity utilization, though not at the same rate as the supply chain lead time. Beyond the 90% utilization level, the gain in capacity cost pales in comparison to the increase in lead time and inventory level.

Focusing on efficiency through economies of scale in ordering, manufacturing, and other supply chain activities too leads to decrease in frequency of shipments, which leads to increase in inventory and lead times. Imagine that

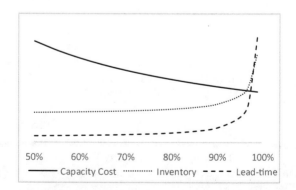

Figure 4.1 The costs of high utilization

a manufacturer's requirement for some input material is 10,000 units every month. For economies in ordering, if the entire quantity required for the month is made available at the beginning of the month in one shipment, the manufacturer's average inventory of this material would be 5,000 units, and the material is available on an average 15 days before its actual requirement. However, if the material were procured in lots of 1000 units every three days, then the manufacturer's average inventory of this material would be 500 units, and the material is available on an average 1.5 days before its actual requirement.

When a firm doing business in the US procures its inputs from distant China, it may save on the landed cost of material (efficiency) but may also end up witnessing a drastic increase in its supply chain lead time. In many instances of outsourcing and offshoring, firms have only considered the reduction in material cost. They have not factored in the increase in uncertainty owing to the lead time becoming longer. In fact, instead of outsourcing production to low-cost countries, like most fashion brands have resorted to, Zara continues to operate its own factories in Spain, which enables it to transact in small batches and have the latest trends in its stores in a matter of a few days.[9]

While it may be true that buyer bargaining power helps lower material costs, it is also interesting to observe the way firms cultivate this bargaining power. Big firms use their scale of purchasing to acquire buyer bargaining power. However, in other firms, the bargaining power is often achieved by committing business well in advance. As the supplier's order book is hardly filled when a buyer contracts six to 12 months in advance, the bargaining power is more with the buyer. In fact, it is a common practice among many suppliers to give significant discounts for orders received well in advance and in large quantities. What the buyers fail to realize while placing orders too early is that they do not have sufficient information about the actual requirement of the material being ordered.

In summary, an "efficiency only" supply chain, while enabling reduction in material, labour, and transport costs, typically operates with long supply chain lead times and is exposed to high levels of demand and supply side uncertainties. Hence, it is ideal only if the product in question has a very stable demand and can be supplied to the market without any supply side uncertainties.

Intangible losses and SCM as a competitive advantage

In the forecasting chapter, we discussed how a supply chain with a longer lead time would be compelled to forecast its demand earlier, which would result in lower forecasting accuracy. Imagine a home goods retailer trying to forecast the sale of air conditioners for the month of April. The April sales forecast, if conducted in March (lead time is one month), February (lead time is two months), and January (lead time is three months) of the same year would have been 900, 1150, and 1500, respectively. The actual demand in April turns out to be 1000. The retailer is able to negotiate a lower unit procurement cost if the order is placed earlier (owing to lead time being longer). The unit procurement cost is £560, £600, and £620 when ordered in January, February, and March, respectively. The retailer procurement quantity is strictly as per forecast, and there is no scope for additional replenishment during the month. The unit selling price of the product is £700, and the leftover at the end of the month is cleared at a unit clearance price of £400. In which month should the retailer order for April sales if it wishes to maximize its profit?

If only the unit procurement cost is considered, the retailer should order in January when the unit procurement cost is least. This type of managerial decision making, where the concerned manager factors only the most relevant cost aspect, described by many experts as local optimal or sub-optimal decision, is a common practice in supply chains. Let us see what the effect of forecasting errors would be depending on when the ordering is carried out. The calculations are as shown in Table 4.1.

Referring to Table 4.1, we see that though the revenue is highest for January ordering and least for March ordering, the profit is highest for March ordering and least for January ordering. This is explained by the forecasting errors owing to when the ordering was done. The forecast errors, absolute

Table 4.1 Illustration of supply chain intangible losses

	Forecast and ordering in:		
	January	*February*	*March*
Unit cost of procurement (£)	560	600	620
Procurement quantity	1500	1150	900
Total cost of procurement (£)	840,000	690,000	558,000
Actual sales at £700	1000	1000	900
Revenue from sales at £700	700,000	700,000	630,000
Leftover at end of April	500	150	0
Revenue on clearance at £400	200,000	60,000	0
Total revenue (£)	900,000	760,000	630,000
Actual Profit (£)	60,000	70,000	72,000
Loss from under-forecasting (£)	–	–	8,000
Loss from over-forecasting (£)	80,000	30,000	–
Intangible Loss (£)	80,000	30,000	8,000

deviation from actual demand, are 500 (over-forecast), 150 (over-forecast), and 100 (under-forecast) in January, February, and March, respectively. The retailer doesn't profit on these quantities. When over-forecast happens, the forecast error quantity becomes leftover inventory and has to be cleared at a loss. The unit losses owing to over-forecasting in January and February are £160 (i.e., 560–400) and £200 (i.e., 600–400), respectively. When under-forecast happens, the forecast error quantity becomes a stock-out loss and is an opportunity loss. The unit loss owing to under-forecasting in March is £80 (i.e., 700–620). The overall loss owing to over- and under-forecasting is obtained by multiplying the unit loss with the respective forecast error quantity.

The losses owing to over- and under-forecasting explain why ordering in March turns out to be more profitable despite the unit cost of procurement being highest. Why is it that it is not common practice to see firms taking their decisions as described in Table 4.1? The primary explanation is the quote attributed to the famous management guru Peter Drucker that "if you can't measure it, you can't manage it." Firms rarely measure the sales they lost owing to insufficient inventory. Even if a firm were to measure lost sales, they do not have to report it to their shareholders. Similarly, if the investor focus is on revenue rather than profitability, it incentivizes managers to oversupply goods and clear unsold goods at a loss. In other words, the consequences of over- or under-forecasting are not easy to measure and typically do not catch the attention of shareholders. Losses from clearance sales are often termed as market losses and looked at as inevitable to doing business. Thus, one could term such losses as intangible losses, and managers give less importance to them vis-à-vis more tangible measures like procurement, production, labour, energy, and transportation costs. Another explanation for intangible losses is the local optimal manner of decision making in organizations. In the preceding illustration, a procurement manager, whose performance is measured on how efficiently material is procured, will obviously choose to procure in January only.

Firms looking at SCM as a competitive advantage most certainly must devote greater attention to minimizing the intangible losses. Particularly when faced with uncertainties on demand or supply, it is not enough to be focussed only on efficiency. Equally important is to focus on customer-centric effectiveness. According to an Ivey Business School case study,[10] despite its manufacturing costs typically being 20% more than those of its rivals procuring from low-cost countries, Zara maintains a handsome profitability compared to its competitors. The reliance on factories close to the market, production in line with demand (close to 85% of the sales in a month were based on production that month itself), and frequent shipments in small batches enable the firm to operate in very short lead times. As a result, Zara boasts a much lower percentage of over- and under-production compared to its rivals. It is interesting to note that owing to its greater orientation towards its customers, Zara stores score higher on the average number of visits by a customer despite spending far lesser than its rivals on advertising.

Responsive supply chains

Hau Lee of Stanford Graduate School of Business defines responsive supply chains as ones "that utilize strategies aimed at being responsive and flexible to the changing and diverse needs of the customers. To be responsive, companies use build-to-order and mass customization processes as a means to meet the specific requirements of customers."[11] Dell going online in 1996 is a classic example of a responsive supply chain. By allowing customers to configure their PCs and track their orders online, Dell created a supply chain where procurement, assembly, and shipping of the customized PC could be executed typically within two weeks' time.[12] The Asian Paints delayed differentiation described in the forecasting chapter is another example of a responsive supply chain. The Asian Paints retailer tints a customized colour after getting a firm order from the customer. This enables the firm to offer an extremely high level of customization without carrying a high level of inventory. More important, the firm is able to respond well to the variations in customer demand.

Agile supply chains

Lee also defines agile supply chains as ones "that utilize strategies aimed at being responsive and flexible to customer needs, while the risks of supply shortages or disruptions are hedged by pooling inventory or other capacity resources." The Zara supply chain, explained in an earlier section, is an apt example of an agile supply chain. Another case that has been well studied is the HP Deskjet printer case, where HP postponed the localization step for their printers (to suit country-specific needs) from their factory to distribution, creating a responsive and agile supply chain.[13] In another case, semiconductor company Xilinx Inc., which faces a highly uncertain demand for semiconductor chips, has adopted a decoupling point strategy such that fabricated wafers are stocked at the decoupling points and final assembly and testing of chips are carried out by other supply chain partners once the demand for specific chips is known from customers, such as Cisco, Dell, HP, and others.[14]

Strategic insights

- Supply chain management still means just improving efficiency and reducing cost for many firms. "Efficiency only" supply chains enhance capacity utilization and provide economies in various supply chain activities. They are ideal only for products or goods that have stable demand and low variation in supply.
- The virtues of "efficiency only" supply chains are at the cost of high inventory levels and long supply chain lead times. Long lead times, accompanied by high uncertainties, contribute to high intangible losses in the form of stock-out losses, clearance sale losses, and inventory losses. These losses are difficult to measure, and minimizing them is not assigned as much importance as reducing more tangible expenses, like procurement, production, and transportation costs.
- Measuring and managing intangible losses is critical to building a competitive advantage on supply chain management for any firm challenged by demand and supply uncertainties, as well as offering high product variety.
- Instead of focussing only on efficiency, excellent supply chains emphasize service and customer effectiveness along with efficiency. They are also better than average firms in understanding and minimizing intangible losses. By investing in responsive or agile supply chains, they ensure higher profitability than supply chains with just efficiency focus.

Notes

1 Ladd, B. 2018. *Playing to Its Strengths: Why Walmart Must Focus on Its Stores and Logistics*. www.forbes.com/sites/brittainladd/2018/09/09/playing-to-its-strengths-why-walmart-must-focus-on-groceries-stores-and-logistics
2 O'Marah, K. 2016. *Zara Uses Supply Chain to Win Again*. www.forbes.com/sites/kevinomarah/2016/03/09/zara-uses-supply-chain-to-win-again
3 Heubusch, J. 2011. *Ronald Reagan's Enduring Economic Legacy*. www.forbes.com/2011/02/08/ronald-reagan-economics-taxes-opinions-contributors-john-heubusch.html
4 Groom, B. 2013. *Industrialists Split Over Thatcher Legacy*. www.ft.com/content/959ebdda-a2cf-11e2-bd45-00144feabdc0
5 Freidman, T. 2005. *The World Is Flat*. New York: Farrar, Straus and Giroux.
6 Basker, E. 2007. The causes and consequences of Wal-Mart's growth. *Journal of Economic Perspectives*, 21(3), 177–198.
7 *Maruti Asks Vendors to Cut Input Costs, Have Own R&D*. www.livemint.com/Companies/Q5ExX79TZXboamI5zuJzoI/Maruti-asks-vendors-to-cut-input-costs-have-own-RampD.html
8 Zachariah, R. 2004. *M S Banga – The Eternal Diplomat*. www.business-standard.com/article/management/m-s-banga-the-eternal-diplomat-104041701003_1.html

9 *Keeping It Under Your Hat*. www.economist.com/business/2016/04/16/keeping-it-under-your-hat
10 Doiron, D. J. 2015. *What Business Is Zara in?* Ivey Business School Case. W15431. London, Canada: Ivey Publishing.
11 Lee, H. L. 2002. Aligning supply chain strategies with product uncertainties. *California Management Review*, 44(3), 105–119.
12 Rangan, V. K., & Bell, M. 1998. *Dell Online*. Harvard Business School Case 598–116.
13 Feitzinger, E., & Lee, H. L. 1997. Mass customization at Hewlett-Packard: The power of postponement. *Harvard Business Review*, 75, 116–123.
14 Lee, H. L. 2002. Aligning supply chain strategies with product uncertainties. *California Management Review*, 44(3), 105–119.

5 Supply chain coordination, contracts, and integration

The bullwhip effect and supply chain coordination

The bullwhip effect has been affecting firms for years. It is the increase in information distortion as one moves up the supply chain from customer end to manufacturer end. The bullwhip symbolizes the length of the supply chain in terms of number of tiers and lead time. The greater the supply chain length, the greater is the bullwhip effect. Whang and Lee explain that the information distortion owing to the bullwhip effect "leads to excessive inventory throughout the system, poor product forecasts, insufficient or excessive capacities, product unavailability, and higher costs generally."[2]

Supply chain coordination implies how coordinated the various stages in a supply chain are with the overall objectives of the chain, which include maximizing the supply chain profit as well as the end customer satisfaction. In fact, these objectives are often interconnected strongly, with the reduction of one leading to the reduction of the other. We defined supply chain management in Chapter 1 as *efficient and effective coordination of material and information flows among suppliers, manufacturers, distributors, and customers so that a wide variety of products could be delivered quickly while keeping costs as low as possible*. Hence, at an operational level, the coordination also implies whether material flow is aligned with the information flow and whether the information flow is in line with the customer requirements. Obviously, the bullwhip effect has a significant role in how well supply chains are coordinated.

At the operational level, apart from a higher number of supply chain tiers and long lead times, one could also identify issues like forecasting buffers (as a hedge against uncertainty), batching, and price fluctuations as contributors to the bullwhip effect. A typical forecasting buffer illustration is one of a manufacturer jacking up the input received from the retailer by 20% under the belief that the retailer may be giving a lower estimate of demand. If the retailer itself had incorporated a 20% buffer, the manufacturer's forecast would be higher by over 40% as a result of the buffers at both tiers. Large batch sizes aggravate the bullwhip effect, as they decrease the frequency of orders between various stages of the supply chain. This results in greater distortion of information and opaqueness in the supply chain. If prices of raw material consumed were to fluctuate widely, a firm could be tempted to stock higher at times when it feels that raw material prices are lower. This too leads to information distortion and opaqueness in the chain.

Drivers of the bullwhip effect

It is however important for a supply chain manager to understand what drives decisions that lead to the bullwhip effect. Had the consequences of the bullwhip effect been easy to measure and associate with the factors contributing to the same, managers would have been successful in containing it. Obviously, there are difficulties in measuring the bullwhip effect and associating them with the drivers. What could be some of the key drivers of the bullwhip effect in supply chains? One major driver of the bullwhip effect is, of course, the efficiency focus that we described in supply chains in the previous chapter. We also described the drawbacks of an "efficiency only" supply chain, which includes large batch sizes, high inventory, supply chain lead time, and uncertainties (both demand and supply).

Another major driver of the bullwhip effect is the way a supply chain is organized and its performance measures are designed. Firms are typically organized functionally, whereby there are separate functions in charge of planning, procurement, production, logistics, distribution, and sales. Despite the advances in information technology and the consequent lowering of organizational barriers to information flow, one notices coordination issues even today, whether it is between different functions of a firm or in transactions between different firms in a supply chain.

The coordination issues emanate from conflicting performance measures that drive different functions. For instance, the procurement function would be measured on how best it minimizes the unit procurement cost. This often leads to bulk procurement and procurement well in advance, so as to extract favourable deals from suppliers, though the firm may not have a clear picture of what its procurement requirements are at the time it takes the procurement decision. The tendency to seek low-cost suppliers from distant locations is also driven by a goal of minimizing unit procurement cost. One notices similar decision-making tendencies in other functions too. A functional organization tends to create silos within the organization. The conflicting goals of the different functions typically create a situation where there is significant competition between the functions instead of a system of cooperation. According to McKinsey, "the inability of functional groups to understand their impact on one another is the most common barrier to collaboration for resolving the major supply chain trade-offs."[3] The same study lists supply chain versus sales, supply chain versus service, and supply chain versus product proliferation as three tensions observed commonly in supply chains.

Centralized versus decentralized supply chains

Just as there are barriers to information flows within an organization owing to conflicting performance measures, there are barriers to coordination between firms in a supply chain owing to differences in the objectives among them. For instance, while a manufacturing firm in the supply chain may be targeting high production or a market share goal, the retailer in the same supply chain could be pursuing a margin maximization goal. In addition, in many supply chains, one firm could be dominant, and the supply chain objectives could be set based on the bargaining power of different entities. For instance, as a dominant entity in its supply chain, Amazon sets the various terms and conditions of trade, leaving very few options for its suppliers.[4] A supply chain where decisions (for instance, the retail price) are based on the interests of individual firms is termed a decentralized supply chain.

Consider a product supply chain comprising a manufacturer and a retailer. Let the product demand be equal to $100 - p$ (to indicate demand reduction with respect to price increase), where p is the retail price. The cost of manufacturing each unit is 40. If the manufacturer sells each unit at 60 to the retailer, the profits of each supply chain partner for three retail prices (60, 70, and 80) are described in Table 5.1. The manufacturer and retail profits are maximized at retail prices of 60 and 80, respectively. These are examples of decentralized supply chains. Depending on who has greater bargaining

Table 5.1 Maximizing supply chain profit

	Retail price (p)		
	60	*70*	*80*
Retail demand, $d = 100 - p$	40	30	20
Retailer revenue ($p \times d$)	2400	2100	1600
Manufacturer revenue ($60 \times d$)	2400	1800	1200
Retailer profit	0	300	**400**
Manufacturer cost ($40 \times d$)	1600	1200	800
Manufacturer profit	**800**	600	400
Supply chain profit	800	**900**	800
Beneficiary	Manufacturer	Supply chain	Retailer

power, the retail price would be set either at 60 or 80. However, had the manufacturer and retailer together been one firm only, we would notice that the profit of the joint entity would be maximized at a retail price of 70. We define the term *supply chain profit* to denote the sum of the profits made by the supply chain members. At a retail price of 70, the supply chain profit is 900, which is greater than the supply chain profit of 800 for retail prices of 60 or 80. A supply chain in which decision making maximizes the collective objectives of the supply chain members is termed a centralized supply chain.

It may be noted in this illustration that though the supply chain profit is maximized for a retail price of 70, *the individual profits of either supply chain member is lower at this price compared to other scenarios.* Hence, a centralized supply chain does not automatically translate into a supply chain that maximizes the individual objectives of the supply chain members. Given this description of a centralized supply chain, one may want to pose the question that if the supply chain member with the greatest power in a supply chain is better off when the supply chain is decentralized (refer to the retailer in Table 5.1 at the retail price 80), then why would such a member be interested in centralization?

A centralized supply chain implies that the members of the supply chain strive for a collective goal, which in turn contributes to a better coordinated supply chain. The relevance of the centralized supply chain concept is to establish the argument that supply chain members working for common goals can achieve higher coordination among themselves through those common goals. (They would do this if each could get a share of the additional economic gains. We will discuss some of the mechanisms to ensure this later.) The common or collective goals could be overall cost or lead-time reduction, overall profit maximization, and end customer satisfaction maximization, among others. When firms in a supply chain have similar objectives, it means that many of their operational decisions should also be aligned with each other, contributing to a high coordination at the operational level too. For instance, if lead-time minimization is a common goal, then operating with small batch sizes would automatically be a common goal. Thus, a centralized supply chain is beneficial to all the supply chain members in the long run. It can thus be said that a collaborative and long-term relationship, rather than an arm's length relationship, is a distinguishing feature of a highly coordinated supply chain.

Coordination through supply chain contracts

Though firms have been aware of the virtues of long-term collaboration and coordination between supply chain members for a while, their implementation has been anything but easy. Developing a framework that truly coordinates the supply chain partners continues to be a challenge to firms across geographies and across industries. In this regard, supply chain contracts have received significant attention in recent times. Through appropriate incentives, a supply chain contract between two supply chain members helps in synchronizing decision making, particularly in the context of various uncertainties in a supply chain.[5] A well-designed supply chain contract enables (i) sharing of risk among the supply chain members; (ii) decision making mirroring that of a centralized supply chain, though ownerships continue to be distinct; and (iii) high supply chain coordination between the supply chain members. It may be noted that the higher the uncertainties in a supply chain, the lower would be the coordination, and a scenario where the risk owing to uncertainty is borne only by one or a few of the supply chain members leads to greater distortion of information flow (members' decisions vis-à-vis actual customer requirements) and further deterioration of the coordination. With the help of the following scenario, we describe the benefits a supply chain can achieve through some of the popular supply contracts.

Imagine a television manufacturer who has launched a new model that would be sold at $500. The direct cost of assembling and distributing each television is $300. The manufacturer sells each television at $400 to the retail firm. The risk arising from demand uncertainty is borne solely by the retail firm. Any television that is left over at the end of the season would be cleared off at $200 per television by the retail firm. The retailer expects the demand to be 1000, 1500, and 2000 units in low, medium, and high demand scenarios, respectively. Based on its own survey, the retailer expects the low, medium, and high demand scenarios to have a likelihood of 35%, 40%, and 25%, respectively. Given the unit costs of overstocking (which is $400 − $200 = $200) and understocking (which is $500 − $400 = $100), using the single period inventory model (refer to Chapter 2), the retailer would find it optimal to order only 1000 television sets from the manufacturer and earn an expected profit of $100,000. Owing to the demand risk, the retailer order is well below the expected demand of 1450 units ($1000 \times 0.35 + 1500 \times 0.40 + 2000 \times 0.25$). The expected profit calculations are shown in Table 5.2.

We have already described the calculations regarding expected sales, leftover, and profit while describing service level (refer to Chapter 2). Using the same definitions, the expected values for a retailer order of 1500 is shown in the following.

Expected sales $= 1000 \times 0.35 + 1500 \times 0.40 + 1500 \times 0.25 = 1325$
Expected leftover $= 500 \times 0.35 + 0 \times 0.40 + 0 \times 0.25 = 175$
Expected retailer profit $= 1325 \times 500 + 175 \times 200 - 1500 \times 400 = \$97,500$

Table 5.2 Expected profits when there is no coordinating supply contract

Retailer order	Expected							
	Retailer						Manufacturer	
	Sales	Sales revenue	Leftover	Clearance revenue	Total revenue	Profit	Sales revenue	Profit
1000	1000	500,000	0	0	500,000	**100,000**	400,000	**100,000**
1500	1325	662,500	175	35,000	697,500	97,500	600,000	150,000
2000	1450	725,000	550	110,000	835,000	35,000	800,000	200,000

We can see that though the manufacturer benefits most with a retailer order of 2000, it is forced to settle for a profit of $100,000 owing to the conservative order by the retailer. Can the manufacturer offer incentives in the form of supply contracts to make the retailer order more?

Had the television manufacturer been an integrated enterprise taking care of both production and sales, it may be noted that as per the single period inventory model calculations, the unit costs of overstocking and understocking would have been $100 (which is $300 – $200) and $200 (which is $500 – $300), respectively, resulting in an order size of 1500 and an integrated enterprise profit of $247,500 (1325 × 500 + 175 × 200 – 1500 × 300).

Buyback contract

To induce the retailer to order more, the manufacturer offers the retailer a buyback contract that assures buyback of unsold television sets at a price higher than the clearance sales price. This incentivizes the retailer to order more. In the preceding example, let the manufacturer offer to buy back any unsold television sets at $300. The new unit costs of overstocking and understocking would be $100 (which is $400 – $300) and $100 (which is $500 – $400), respectively, for which the retailer would find it optimal to order 1500 television sets from the manufacturer. The expected profit calculations are shown in the following table (Table 5.3).

As we can see from the table, the buyback offer induces the retailer to order 1500 units for which its expected profit is $115,000 ($15,000 more than with no buyback contract). The manufacturer has to bear a loss of $100 (which is $300 – $200) on every unit bought back from the manufacturer. However, since the retailer has placed a larger order, the profit of the manufacturer is still higher at $132,500 ($32,500 more than with no buyback contract). The profit of the manufacturer and retailer together is $247,500, which we saw would have been the profit had the business been an integrated enterprise. Thus, the buyback contract helps the decentralized supply chain to transit to a centralized supply chain.

Table 5.3 Buyback contract

Retailer order	Expected						Manufacturer		
	Retailer								
	Sales	Sales revenue	Leftover	Clearance revenue	Total revenue	Profit	Sales revenue	Loss on clearance	Profit
1000	1000	500,000	0	0	500,000	100,000	400,000	0	100,000
1500	1325	662,500	175	52,500	715,000	**115,000**	600,000	17,500	**132,500**
2000	1450	725,000	550	165,000	890,000	90,000	800,000	55,000	145,000

Revenue sharing contract

In a revenue sharing contract, for a revenue share, the manufacturer offers a discount in the price at which it sells the product to the retailer. Let the manufacturer offer a contract such that 10% of the sales at $500 is shared by the retailer with the manufacturer. Thus, for each television sold at $500, the retailer earns $450 and the manufacturer earns $50. In return, the manufacturer sells each television to the retailer at $350 instead of at $400. The new unit costs of overstocking and understocking would be $150 (which is $350 – $200) and $100 (which is $450 – $350), respectively, for which the retailer would find it optimal to order 1500 television sets from the manufacturer. The expected profit calculations are shown in Table 5.4.

As we can see from the table, the revenue share offer induces the retailer to order 1500 units for which its expected profit is $106,250 ($6250 more than with no revenue share contract). The manufacturer earns only $350 on each television sold to the retailer, though it earns $50 through revenue share on every unit sold at $500 by the retailer. Thus, the profit of the manufacturer is still higher at $141,250 ($41,250 more than with no revenue share contract). The profit of the manufacturer and retailer together is $247,500, which is what we saw would have been the profit had the business been an integrated enterprise. Thus, the revenue sharing contract helps the decentralized supply chain to transit to a centralized supply chain.

Sales rebate contract

In a sales rebate contract, the manufacturer offers a rebate in the price at which it sells the product to the retailer for the retailer order that is above a particular level. In the television example, let the manufacturer offer a rebate of $50 for the retailer order that is above 1000. The retailer would find it optimal to order 1500 television sets from the manufacturer. The expected profit calculations are shown in Table 5.5.

As we can see from the table, the sales rebate offer induces the retailer to order 1500 units for which its expected profit is $122,500 ($22,500 more than with no sales rebate contract). The profit of the manufacturer is still higher at $125,000 ($25,000 more than with no sales rebate contract). The profit of the manufacturer and retailer together is $247,500, which is what we saw would have been the profit had the business been an integrated enterprise. Thus, the sales rebate contract helps the decentralized supply chain to transit to a centralized supply chain.

Table 5.4 Revenue sharing contract

Retailer order	Expected						Manufacturer		
	Retailer								
	Sales	Sales revenue	Leftover	Clearance revenue	Total revenue	Profit	Sales revenue	Share of retail sale	Profit
1000	1000	450,000	0	0	450,000	100,000	350,000	50,000	100,000
1500	1325	596,250	175	35,000	631,250	**106,250**	525,000	66,250	**141,250**
2000	1450	652,500	550	110,000	762,500	62,500	700,000	72,500	172,500

Table 5.5 Sales rebate contract

Retailer order	Expected							Manufacturer		
	Retailer									
	Sales	Sales revenue	Leftover	Clearance revenue	Total revenue	Profit		Sales rebate	Sales revenue	Profit
1000	1000	500,000	0	0	500,000	100,000		0	400,000	100,000
1500	1325	662,500	175	35,000	697,500	**122,500**		25,000	575,000	**125,000**
2000	1450	725,000	550	110,000	835,000	85,000		50,000	750,000	150,000

Other contracts

The contracts discussed earlier are predicated on certain conditions. The revenue sharing contract for example is based on the assumption that the manufacturer has perfect information about the retailer's revenues or that the retailer accurately shares its revenue information with the manufacturer. Further, the implementation of each contract also varies. Revenue sharing between supply chain partners for example can be implemented in a case where sales at the retailer's end can be tracked through advanced information systems. Further, a buyback contract may not be applicable for perishable goods but has seen widespread applications in case of new product introductions or books. In case of a new product introduction, a buyback contract provides the manufacturer with an opportunity to incentivize the retailer to order more and provide more shelf space to the new product and in turn reduce the retailer's risk by allowing buyback of unsold stocks.

Often, however, information asymmetry exists between supply chain entities and may bring forth challenges in coordination. Studies have shown that specially designed contracts, such as capacity reservation contracts or advance purchase contracts, can help align decisions of supply chain partners. Consider the context of a supplier who requires the acquisition of necessary capacity before receiving an order from the manufacturer. In the case of private forecast information of the manufacturer, there are alternatives to coordinate the supply chain. The manufacturer can pay a fee to reserve capacity or place an order before the supplier secures capacity. In both these cases, even under information asymmetry, the manufacturer's actions provide a signal that allows the supplier to purchase capacity. There are several other contract designs such as the two-part tariff, consignment, and quantity flexibility contracts that are in use in different industry sectors.

The success of a contract in aligning the decisions of supply chain players, however, lies in sharing supply chain risks and providing a win-win situation for supply chain partners.

Supply chain integration

While supply chain coordination refers to how well the material and information flows are coordinated between various stages in a supply chain to meet the overall objectives of the chain, it assumes that each firm in the supply chain is an independent entity. It relies on incentivizing instruments like supply chain contracts to achieve the coordination. Given their transactional nature, there are limits to how well two members in a chain can be integrated through contracts. Supply chain integration refers to a greater degree of association between members of a supply chain than through supply chain coordination, though its objectives are very similar to supply chain coordination. It involves creation of common resources like information systems or joint ventures and at a strategic level could even imply an integration through ownership. Hence, one could argue that supply chain integration is a longer-term and more strategic intervention compared to an intervention like a supply chain contract. No doubt, supply chain integration is a distinct feature of many successful supply chains.

Supply chain integration through information technology (IT) systems

One of the best cited instances of supply chain integration through IT systems is that of Dell Computers.[6] Michael Dell described it as virtual integration, which was the integration of the Dell customer with all the other entities of the Dell supply chain through IT systems. It meant that an order from customer for a customized computer was instantaneously shared with the Dell suppliers so that components are delivered to the Dell factory only after knowing customer demand. The Dell factory in turn was a fast assembly system, integrated with the Dell IT system, which operated on a made to order (MTO, refer to Chapter 3) basis. Virtual integration ensured that a finished computer was ready to be shipped from the Dell factory within 36 hours of receiving the order from the customer. The finished computers were typically received by the customers in a matter of seven to ten days' time. With virtual integration, Michael Dell argued that inventory could be substituted by information, helping supply chains to drastically cut their lead times. Another example of a supply chain integration through IT is the Walmart CPFR that we described in Chapter 3.

While the flow of information within a firm is technologically well advanced, thanks to ERP software, the same between firms in a supply chain is still an area with significant scope for improvement. In transactions between firms, the most advanced mode presently is where a supplier firm ERP system has access to the buyer firm's ERP system, based on which the supplier takes decisions on ordering, shipping, and inventory level. However, such decision making still comes with a high amount of human intervention. Other than some instances of automated replenishment in some large global manufacturers, "few procurement processes are fully automated and end-to-end information transparency is limited."[7] According to Steve Smith, the US COO of Esker S.A. (a documentation processing automation solution provider), "the challenges in the supply chain are made more daunting because sales order processing in many ways is still a highly manual operation." He argues that a migration from manual processing to an automated customer order management software would result, among others, in substantial supply chain visibility increase and customer experience improvement.[8]

Many concepts in recent years like "artificial intelligence," "digital supply chains," "end-to-end supply chain management (e2e SCM)," and "machine learning," to name a few, are expected to contribute to the migration from manual processing to automated processing. It may be noted that the argument in favour of automation is not to make human beings redundant but to transit towards the highest level of coordination between material and information flows among various firms in a supply chain.

Supply chain integration through partnerships

In addition to integration through IT systems, firms have been exploring the benefits of integration through different forms of partnerships. Such partnerships include vendor managed inventory (VMI), third party logistics (3PL), and long-term supplier alliances. One of the best cited VMI partnerships is the one between Procter & Gamble and Walmart. As the term indicates, the supplier manages the inventory at the buyer end. This helps reduce the information barrier between the buyer and supplier, which in turn improves the supply chain coordination. 3PL partnerships, which have increased vastly in the past few decades, refer to the outsourcing of various supply chain activities, like packing, transportation, warehousing, and distribution. The easy tracking of material and orders that is facilitated by 3PL firms ensures that supply chain coordination is not affected despite the outsourcing of these activities to an external entity. Supplier alliances are relevant since a significant proportion of manufacturing activities have been outsourced in recent decades. A supplier alliance of interest in recent times is that of Apple with Foxconn. Many of these supplier alliances focus on achieving a level of supply chain coordination that is on par with what would have been there had there been no outsourcing. This is described in more detail in the "Strategic Supplier Partnerships" section in the next chapter.

Supply chain integration through vertical integration

While sticking to core competency and outsourcing non-core activities have been characteristics of many supply chains in the latter part of the last century and the beginning of this century, there have also been certain business examples that are in contradiction with industry practice. Walmart and recently Amazon are examples of integrated retailers who apart from the traditional retailing activity are also present in various other supply chain activities like procurement, transportation, warehousing, and even in manufacturing. Other examples of firms that are an exception to the outsourcing trend are furniture company IKEA, electric car manufacturer Tesla, and apparel firm Zara.[9] The movement towards closely integrating supply chain activities is against the popular notion of outsourcing. However, closer analysis of such firm strategies show that integrated supply chains provide better control of supply chain activities and an ability to quickly react to uncertainties.

Strategic insights

- The bullwhip effect, an indicator of how poorly a supply chain is coordinated, is high in "efficiency only" supply chains and manifests as large batch sizes, high inventory, long supply chain lead times, and huge variations in supply.
- A functional supply chain organization structure with performance measures of functions conflicting with performance measures of other functions or a supply chain where different firms pursue conflicting goals experiences a significant bullwhip effect.
- Excellent firms focus on aligning the performance measures of various functions so that organizational conflict and bullwhip effect are minimized, and supply chain performance is maximized.
- Excellent supply chains focus on supply chain coordination through effective supply chain contracts or through supply chain integration. A well-designed supply chain contract ensures (i) sharing of risk among the supply chain partners and (ii) decision making to mirror that of a centralized supply chain.

Notes

1 Lee, H. L., Padmanabhan, V., & Whang, S. 1997. The bullwhip effect in supply chains. *Sloan Management Review*, 38, 93–102.
2 Reese, J. 1995. *Whang and Lee: Eliminating the Bullwhip Effect in Supply Chains.* www.gsb.stanford.edu/insights/whang-lee-eliminating-bullwhip-effect-supply-chains
3 Glatzel, C., Grosspietsch, J., & Silva, I. 2011. Is your top team undermining your supply chain? *Supply Chain Management Review*, 15(6).
4 Soper, S. 2018. *Amazon Is Squeezing Suppliers to Curb Losses in Price Wars.* www.bloomberg.com/news/articles/2018–03–20/amazon-is-said-to-squeeze-suppliers-to-curb-losses-in-price-wars
5 Narayanan, V. G., & Raman, A. 2004. Aligning incentives in supply chains. *Harvard Business Review*, 82(11), 94–102.
6 Magretta, J. 1998. The power of virtual integration: An interview with Dell Computer's Michael Dell. *Harvard Business Review*, 76(2), 73–84.
7 Evans, H., & Easton, S. *The Future of Procurement Arrives at Last.* www.atkearney.com/procurement/article?/a/the-future-of-procurement-arrives-at-last
8 Smith, S. 2018. *Manufacturers and Automated Order Processing: The Benefits.* www.manufacturing.net/article/2018/01/manufacturers-and-automated-order-processing-benefits
9 *Keeping It Under Your Hat.* www.economist.com/business/2016/04/16/keeping-it-under-your-hat

6 Procurement and vendor management

Procurement and vendor management are critical aspects of SCM. In its early years, SCM used to be highly dominated by procurement and supply management. As procurement expense is roughly about 60% to 70% of the sales revenue in most manufacturing firms, it is also typically the top expense item. Hence, a 10% savings in procurement cost contributes more to the overall cost reduction than a 10% savings in any another expense item. On a stand-alone basis, firms have made great strides in improving procurement efficiency. However, as mentioned in previous chapters, becoming more efficient on procurement (for instance through outsourcing) is often at the cost of reducing the supply chain's effectiveness or increasing the supply chain uncertainty. Hence, it is very important to integrate procurement and vendor management with the firm's supply chain objectives. Integration is a common theme in the different aspects we explore in this chapter.

Make or buy?

A question that precedes the procurement decision is whether to make (in-house) or buy (from an outside supplier). As discussed earlier, sticking to core competency and outsourcing non-core activities have been characteristics of many supply chains in the last few decades. In contrast, strong vertical integration was popular in many industries in the early part of the 20th century. Ford Motors was famous at that time for owning even rubber plantations and iron ore mines. Firms in industries like automobiles, petroleum, and steel were present in many more parts of their respective value chains in comparison to the current era. A typical automobile firm made most of the components going into a car in addition to managing the assembly lines.

After the two world wars, industries became more complex to manage as they matured. Simultaneously, good suppliers and supplier networks started emerging, encouraging firms to outsource some of the activities being carried out in-house. Though outsourcing helped in containing costs, the larger motive was in transferring an activity to a firm that specialized in it. It is no wonder that the outsourcing that used to happen till the 1980s was geographically restricted to firms located near to the buyer's plants. The emergence of ancillary firms around Detroit in the USA, Chennai in India, and "Toyota City" near Nagoya in Japan are examples of local outsourcing in the automobile industry. This era also saw the emergence of *keiretsu* (a Japanese word that symbolizes a supplier network), where suppliers and buyers had financial stakes in each other's businesses.[2] Such cross-holdings enabled the supply chains to operate more closely than in usual arm's length-based supply chains. The Toyota keiretsu became world famous for raising quality standards not just within Toyota but across the entire Toyota supply chain comprising itself and all its suppliers.[3]

The globalization wave that emerged in the 1990s heralded large-scale outsourcing that became a phenomenon for the next few decades. Outsourcing was no longer limited to suppliers located in nearby localities. Minimizing the landed cost of goods purchased became the new catchphrase. With international logistics becoming more efficient and less time-consuming, firms embarked on outsourcing with a fervour never seen before. US firms sourcing from Mexico started giving way to sourcing from China. From a manufacturer of athletic shoes in the 1970s, Nike transformed itself into a firm restricted to only designing, testing, and selling by 1985. The entire manufacturing operation had been outsourced to China by then.[4]

However, the "make or buy" question didn't have buy (outsource) as the obvious answer. Many instances of firms suffering owing to excessive outsourcing started emerging. Despite being a pioneer in digital cameras, Kodak could not survive, as outsourcing of its design and production activities knocked out whatever advantages it had over its rivals.[5] Increased subcontracting of design and production contributed to the success of the Boeing 777 product development. However, a still higher level of design and production outsourcing ended up in huge delays in the Boeing 787 Dreamliner product development.[6] It may not be a mere coincidence that Dell lost its US personal computer market leadership (on market share) in 2009, one year after it closed its flagship factory at Round Rock near Austin, Texas, and outsourced production to China like most of its competitors.

The "make or buy" decision is a vital strategic decision that should not be based on a herd instinct. As mentioned in the previous chapter, Zara prides in being a vertically integrated apparel retailer and procures only a small share of its sales from external suppliers. The "make or buy" decision should not be based just on minimizing the landed cost, which may be fine when both demand and supply are stable but should also factor in other aspects like delivery reliability, volume flexibility, quality, lead time, and supply uncertainty when either demand or supply (or both) are volatile. A firm should also factor in the risks of losing knowledge and other advantages through outsourcing to another firm which could eventually turn out to be a competitor or become a supplier to the outsourcing firm's competitor.

ABC analysis

An important tool for any procurement manager is the ABC or spend analysis. As the starting step, the ABC analysis categorizes the items procured by a firm into A, B, and C classes. Items procured by the firm are arranged on the descending order of their total annual spend value. The top 10% of the items that account for about 70% of the total procurement spend are categorized as A items. The next 20% of the items that account for about 20% of the total procurement spend are categorized as B items. The bottom 70% of the items that account for the balance (about 10%) of the total procurement spend are categorized as C items. The next step is to decide different procurement-related decisions for various item purchases based on the class the item belongs to. The typical procurement-related decisions for items belonging to the three classes are as shown in Table 6.1.

As A items account for close to 70% of purchase value, it makes sense to buy them frequently so that working capital held as raw material inventory is not high. This would require the purchases to be in small lot sizes, which would imply that the cycle stock would be low. In many contexts, A items are raw materials that are specific to the buyer's requirements unlike C items, which in many situations are standard or commodity items. For instance, steel sheets of a particular grade required by an automobile maker or specific coal required by a thermal power plant or the compressor required by an air conditioner manufacturer are examples of A items, while the standard fastener is a classic example of a C item.

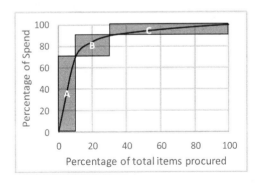

Figure 6.1 ABC or spend analysis

Table 6.1 Procurement decisions for A, B, and C items

Decision	A class	B class	C class
Purchase frequency	Frequently	Regularly	Occasionally
Purchase lot size	Small	Moderate	Large
Cycle stock* (in days)	Low	Medium	High
Safety stock* (in days)	High	Medium	Low
Sourcing rationale	Strategic	Flexibility	Commodity
Vendor relationship	Long-term	Medium-term	Arm's-length
Managerial priority	70%	20%	10%

* Refer to Chapter 2 for a description of cycle stock and safety stock.

This implies that arranging an alternate source would be most difficult for an A item in case of a disruption in supply. Hence, it is prudent to hold high safety stock for A items and for the same reason to pursue a sourcing rationale that is strategic. Being strategic implies that the sourcing rationale would provide a competitive advantage for the buyer vis-à-vis its competitors and could include fostering a long-term relationship with A item vendors.

As B and C items are lower in value and typically easier to manage in case of supply disruptions or shortages, the sourcing rationale need not be strategic. For B items, it may emphasize buyer flexibility, while for C items, a commodity procurement approach would suffice. This implies that a buyer is not required to invest in a long-term relationship for B and C item suppliers and could instead resort to a medium-term and arm's-length relationship, respectively. The analysis also emphasizes that a procurement manager's managerial priorities should also be dictated by the value of the items being procured. This means that A items deserve 70% of the managerial time though they may account only for 10% of the total items being procured!

Supply risk

While the ABC analysis helps a manager to prioritize procurement decisions with greater priority for items that account for a larger share of procurement value (hence, greater impact on the bottom line of the buying firm), it does not factor into the supply risk of various items procured. Some items, irrespective of whether they are A or C, would have a very high supply risk. Broadly, supply risk could be owing to (i) issues pertaining to the supplier firm or industry and (ii) issues pertaining to the environment in which the supplier firm operates.

Supply risk emanating from the supplier firm or industry

This category of supply risk refers to the risk in supply owing to (i) greater demand side pressures on the supplier firm or industry, (ii) the competitive structure of the supplier firm industry, (iii) greater supply side uncertainties associated with the supplier firm, and (iv) location of the supplier firm.

Greater demand side pressure refers to situations when there is a surge in demand which results in supplier firms receiving orders that are close to their production capacities. Once the orders start exceeding 80–90% of supplier capacity, then the ability of the supplier to adhere to the usual lead times and order quantities starts declining. An extended period of demand surge would in addition lead to higher bargaining power for the supplier along with an ability to charge a higher price. The 2014 global solar panel shortage is an instance of higher supply risk owing to a surge in demand.[7]

The competitive structure of the supplier firm industry refers to the extent of choice available with buyer firms to choose from whom they desire to procure goods. The greater the number of suppliers to choose from, the greater is the buyer's bargaining power and the lower the supply risk. A classic example of supplier firm dominance and, hence, buyer plans being dictated by the supplier is the dominance displayed till recently by Intel in supply of computer microchips.[8]

Supply side uncertainties associated with the supplier firm refers to various uncertainties like raw material price fluctuation, raw material shortage, inconsistent quality, production disruptions, and labour shortage or strife. As can be seen, these uncertainties are an outcome of how well managed the supplier firm is. This supply risk would be low in supplier firms that are well managed.

The location of the supplier firm with respect to the buyer firm has a bearing on the risk of material supply. Proximate suppliers can supply in small quantities on a frequent just-in-time basis. Supply by distant suppliers is riskier, as they tend to ship in larger batch sizes for transportation economics. In addition, the greater the distance material must travel, the greater would be the risk associated with the transportation. Toyota City, which was described in the beginning of this chapter, is an example of a buyer initiative to reduce supply risk by having as many suppliers as possible near to the mother plant.

Supply risk emanating from the environment in which the supplier firm operates

This category of supply risk refers to the risk in supply owing to the conditions in which the supplier production facility operates and includes issues like climate variations, natural disasters, political and social stability, availability of skilled labour, tariffs, and trade disputes.

Despite great progress in technology, climate still plays a significant role in affecting supply in several industries. In many geographies, like India and China, there are distinct seasons. Each season could be intense with summer being extremely hot and dry, the rainy season being very wet, and winter seeing heavy snowfalls (as in Alaska, Nordic countries, and Russia). The rainy season affects the output of coal or minerals mined if the mines are opencast. Offshore oil drilling is often affected during hurricane season in many parts of the world. Similarly, winter months in regions with heavy snowfalls witness production and transportation disruption. Production in industries that consume large quantities of water are affected during summer or dry seasons.

Suppliers based in regions that are more prone to natural disasters are categorized as high supply risk unless adequate measures are available to mitigate the impact of such disasters. Japan is an example of a country prone to natural disasters; it manages earthquakes and typhoons without economic activities being affected. However, the disaster that followed the 2011 Tohoku earthquake and tsunami disrupted supply chains not just in Japan but across the world.[9] As the climate warms, there is evidence of extreme rains gaining strength.[10] Extreme rains and rising sea levels are expected to increase the risk of flooding in coastal areas, which is where a lot of supply chain activities like manufacturing and warehousing are located owing to their closeness to sea ports. On this count, many global suppliers based out of the coastal areas of China, Vietnam, Malaysia, Thailand, and Bangladesh carry a moderate to high level of supply risk.

Political and social instability along with industrial strife in the region where a supplier is located goes a long way in enhancing the risk perception of potential buyers. Countries with a dysfunctional democracy or autocratic form of rule have typically scored poorly on political and social stability. The perception of South Korea as a stable supply source strengthened after the establishment of the Sixth Republic in 1987. Argentina and Turkey, despite being democracies, have carried a perception of instability owing to past coup attempts. In India, Kolkata and Mumbai lost their industrial pre-eminence owing to the industrial strife of the 1970s and 1980s. In recent years, Egypt and Pakistan have seen a decline in their fortunes as apparel-exporting countries owing to political instability and terrorism.

Changes to skilled labour availability are another factor contributing to supply risk perception. As a country or a region progresses economically and the share of its service sector in overall GDP increases, the availability of skilled labour in manufacturing and other supply chain activities tightens. This often results in wage increases and higher attrition in jobs, which reduces its attraction as a supplier hub and increases the risk perception. In coming years, the skill shortage will likely get more acute owing to the decline in fertility levels in many industrial nations, which results in a smaller number of people available to replace the older workforce. Signs of this are already visible in ageing countries like Japan, South Korea, China, and Germany.

Supply risk is lower when there is stability in tariff and trade rules. Till the implementation of goods and services tax (GST) in 2017, duties and tax rates used to change regularly in India, forcing firms to make regular changes to their supply chain decisions like where to source production from and where to locate warehouses. The advent of the WTO and the signing of trade deals like the North American Free Trade Agreement (NAFTA) in the 1990s brought greater stability to trade and tariffs. This in turn resulted in greater stability with regard to supply chain decisions. However, the change of government in the US in 2016 has also led to changes in policies, such as the tariff imposition on goods imported from China.[11] Supply chain decisions, especially where material will be procured from, are expected to undergo major changes in the coming years as a result of the increased trends in protectionism and trade wars.

Irrespective of what the risk source is, it is clear from the preceding arguments that low risk implies stable supply. Indirectly, it also implies that the buyer has a greater control of its supply chain. In contrast, a moderate or high supply risk connotes low bargaining power for the buyer. Effective supply chain management means the ability to identify and work with low supply risks and ensure backup arrangements in case of high supply risks. The latter will be discussed in detail in the next chapter.

Procurement strategies

For a considerable stretch of time, procurement strategies were designed primarily based on how much impact the material procured had on the profitability of the buyer firm. In that era, the procurement strategies were basically an outcome of the ABC analysis described earlier. However, firms realized that procurement strategies based just on the profit impact of material procurement had shortcomings and left the firm vulnerable from the viewpoint of competitiveness.

Peter Kraljic proposed an approach to classify all purchased materials or components in terms of profit impact and supply risk, famously known as the Kraljic matrix, and suggested procurement strategies based on which category the material belonged to.[12] The Kraljic matrix is still a vital tool used by industry for designing procurement strategies.[13] As per Kraljic's classification,

the company sorts out all its purchased items into the following categories: **strategic** (high profit impact, high supply risk), **bottleneck** (low profit impact, high supply risk), **leverage** (high profit impact, low supply risk), and **noncritical** (low profit impact, low supply risk).[12]

The procurement approach for each category is described in the following sections.

Strategic items

For strategic items, Kraljic proposes development of long-term supply relationships, contract staggering, and contingency planning.[12] Decision making should be at the top level, like the vice president of purchasing. We describe long-term supply relationships in the section titled "Strategic Supplier Partnerships" later in this chapter.

Bottleneck items

For bottleneck items, Kraljic proposes volume insurance, large inventory buffers, and backup plans.[12] Decision making should be at a higher level, like the department head. Volume insurance implies quantity assurance from the supplier, which may even be at a cost premium. However, since bottleneck items have a low impact on profit, this cost premium or inventory carrying cost would only have a minor impact on buyer profitability.

Leverage items

As discussed earlier, low supply risk implies greater control for the buyer along with better bargaining power. As leverage items have a high profit impact, Kraljic proposes exploitation of full purchasing power by the buyer so that procurement cost is minimized. This would involve proper vendor selection, product substitution, negotiations, fixing the contract/spot purchasing mix, and order volume optimization. Decision making should be at medium level like the chief buyer.[12]

Noncritical items

Finally, for noncritical items, given they have low profit impact as well as supply risk, Kraljic proposes product standardization, order volume and inventory optimization, and efficient processing. Decision making should be at a lower level like the buyer.[12]

Supplier development

When the suppliers available to choose from are not able to deliver at the level expected by the buyer, the buyer must either train them to reach the higher level or invest in a new supplier. This process is described as a supplier development. A buyer may also resort to supplier development if the supply risk of the current suppliers is high (bottleneck or strategic items). Through development of alternate suppliers, it is possible to convert a bottleneck item to noncritical and a strategic item to leverage.

Handfield et. al. describe the experiences of BMW, Daewoo, Honda, Hyundai, and IBM, among others, in employing supplier development.[14] These firms use the services of their own employees to help suppliers facing difficulties. IBM and Daewoo resort to part standardization and vendor rationalization (including use of single sourcing) to achieve supplier economies of scale, which contributes to the business development of the supplier.

When even these support measures prove insufficient, firms could encourage enterprising members of their staff to start off as new suppliers. Depending on the gravity of the situation, this spawning of new suppliers could even be with the infrastructural and financial support of the buyer firm as can be seen from the example of telecom company Bharti Airtel.[15]

Strategic supplier partnerships

The essence of strategic supplier partnerships is about building long-term relationships with suppliers so that the buyer firm can meet its customer expectations on efficiency and effectiveness at the highest level. In a context of low supply risk, which also implies a greater level of supply reliability, the conditions do not warrant the investment in strategic tie-ups with suppliers. As discussed earlier, the need for strategic supplier partnerships is highest when supply risk is moderate or high and the item purchased has a high impact on the buyer's profitability. We look at some well-known examples of time-tested strategic supplier partnerships. Strategic supplier partnerships imply a high level of trust between buyer and supplier, along with long-term business commitment. Instead of viewing the supplier as just a manufacturer of items designed by the buyer, strategic supplier partnerships involve suppliers in understanding the needs of the buyer's customers and in designing and manufacturing the items that they supply. In a strategic partnership, the buyer and supplier firms share common goals in meeting the expectations of the buyer's customers.

In their article on building deep supplier relationships, Liker and Choi contrast the practices of Honda and Toyota with that of Ford, GM, and Chrysler.[16] The authors note that while the Japanese firms, through their keiretsu networks, treated their suppliers with great respect, the American firms often had confrontational relationships with their suppliers. While setting high standards for improvement, the Japanese firms went out of their way to help their suppliers to improve continuously. While the American firms followed a practice of calculating costs and setting the supplier's component price, the Japanese firms figured out the cost suppliers can incur for a given target price so that the suppliers can also earn a decent profit.

The Apple-Foxconn partnership is another famous example of a strategic supplier partnership.[17] According to Kanematsu,

> when it came to the iPhone, Foxconn not only handled production and met tight deadlines but also played a crucial role in realizing Apple's aesthetic vision. It is no exaggeration to say the success of the iPhone depended on Foxconn, and Foxconn's growth hinged on the iPhone.

Both examples highlight the strategic importance of treating suppliers as partners rather than as entities to be exploited (a possibility owing to buyer's bargaining power). A strategic supplier partnership enables the extension of the buyer firm's business objectives to be extended to its network of suppliers too, without any financial stake in the supplier firms. It strives for cost and quality improvements in the material procured such that the benefits of improvement are shared fairly among the partners. A strategic supplier partnership is indeed about carving a win-win relationship!

Strategic insights

- Excellent firms develop their procurement strategies by factoring in both profit impact and supply risk, instead of just the former.
- Long-term strategic supplier partnerships where suppliers are treated as equal partners and both parties share common goals is a hallmark of excellent supply chains.

Notes

1 Tang, C. S., Zimmerman, J. D., & Nelson, J. I. 2009. Managing new product development and supply chain risks: The Boeing 787 case. *Supply Chain Forum: An International Journal*, 10(2), 74–86.
2 *Keiretsu.* www.economist.com/news/2009/10/16/keiretsu
3 Sanger, D. E. 1990. *U.S. Suppliers Get a Toyota Lecture.* www.nytimes.com/1990/11/01/business/us-suppliers-get-a-toyota-lecture.html
4 Srinivasan, B. 2018. *Americana: A 400-year History of American Capitalism.* Penguin.
5 *Kodak: What Led to Bankruptcy.* www.hindustantimes.com/business/kodak-what-led-to-bankruptcy/story-Wgkw8P1YdxSqH60EoZpNhO.html
6 *Herd Instinct.* www.economist.com/special-report/2013/01/19/herd-instinct
7 *Solar Boom Drives First Global Panel Shortage since 2006.* www.livemint.com/Industry/XoB539VaiRzPnJDGgu MkPM/Solar-boom-drives-first-global-panel-shortage-since-2006.html
8 Maskara, S. 2018. *No More 'Intel Inside' says Apple: End of the Microchip Giant's Dominance.* https://qrius.com/no-more-intel-inside-says-apple-end-of-microchip-giants-dominance/

9 Carty, S. S., & Kurtenbach, E. 2011. *Tohuku Disaster may Bring Automakers to their Knees*. www.japantimes.co.jp/news/2011/03/29/business/tohoku-disaster-may-bring-automakers-to-their-knees

10 Witze, A. 2018. *Why Extreme Rains Are Gaining Strength as the Climate Warms*. www.nature.com/articles/d41586-018-07447-1

11 Chen, Y., & Lawder, D. 2018. *China Says Trump Forces Its Hand, Will Retaliate Against New U.S. Tariffs*. www.reuters.com/article/us-usa-trade-china-tariffs/trump-slaps-tariffs-on-200-billion-in-chinese-goods-threatens-267-billion-more-idUSKCN1LX2M3

12 Kraljic, P. 1983. Purchasing must become supply management. *Harvard Business Review*, 61(5), 109–117.

13 Webb, J. 2017. *What Is the Kraljic Matrix?* www.forbes.com/sites/jwebb/2017/02/28/what-is-the-kraljic-matrix

14 Handfield, R. B., Krause, D. R., Scannell, T. V., & Monczka, R. M. 2000. Avoid the pitfalls in supplier development. *Sloan Management Review*, 41(2), 37–49.

15 Abrar, P. 2011. *Corporates like Bharti Airtel, Infosys, Wipro and Microland Help Staff Turn Entrepreneurs*. https://eco nomictimes.indiatimes.com/news/company/corporate-trends/corporates-like-bharti-airtel-infosys-wipro-and-microland-help-staff-turn-entrepreneurs/articleshow/10950489.cms

16 Liker, J., & Choi, T. Y. 2004. Building deep supplier relationships. *Harvard Business Review*, 82(12), 104–113.

17 Kanematsu, Y. 2017. *Foxconn, Apple and the Partnership that Changed the Tech Sector*. https://asia.nikkei.com/Business/Foxconn-Apple-and-the-partnership-that-changed-the-tech-sector

7 Supply chain risk management

While discussing procurement strategies in the previous chapter, we dealt in detail with the risk faced by a firm from its supplier side. However, that is only one of the many risks faced by a firm. Apart from the risk arising from the supplier side, disruptions could be from other supply sources like its own factories or any of the entities in the outbound side of the firm. A firm seeking supply chain excellence also cannot afford to ignore the risks as a result of sudden demand collapse owing to quality issues or external factors.

Economic cost of disruptions

The economic cost of a disruption is often difficult to estimate. A firm operating in a monopolistic situation may find that the loss owing to a disruption is limited to sales loss during the disruption and the cost of resuming production or supply. However, in a competitive situation, the losses go beyond these two aspects. A firm's business could be wiped out, or it could witness significant fall in market share if it were to face disruption while operating in a competitive situation or a situation where its customers could make alternative arrangements.

Ericsson, for example, was forced to exit phone handset production in 2000 after the Albuquerque plant of computer chip supplier Philips Electronics was damaged by a lightning strike. However, its competitor Nokia was affected far less, as it proactively arranged an alternate supply from another supplier. In fact, Nokia converted a calamity into an opportunity owing to Ericsson not having a plan B.[3] In another example, the 2010 explosion and oil spill in one of BP's oil wells in the Gulf of Mexico resulted in penalties and claims beyond \$60 billion, and a 55% drop in shareholder wealth for BP. By 2013, BP dropped to being the fourth largest oil company from second largest.[4] Annual sales of Patanjali Ayurved, an upcoming Indian fast-moving consumer goods (FMCG) company, declined by more than 10% in 2018 as a result of the firm not being prepared for the goods and services tax (GST) that was implemented starting in July 2017.[5] A research study based on a sample of 519 glitch announcements made during 1989–2000 indicates that supply chain glitch announcements were associated with an abnormal decrease in shareholder value of 10.28%.[6]

Supply chain disruptions and risk

Supply chain disruptions can be owing to any disruption on the supply side. It could be a result of disruption at supplier factories, the firm's own factories, distributor points, or retailer outlets. It could also be owing to disruptions in the transportation network. Supply chain disruptions could also occur as a result of sudden changes in demand owing to competitor actions or product innovation. They can be categorized into four categories based on their predictability and disruption intensity: **catastrophic** (low predictability, high disruption intensity), **anticipatable** (high predictability, high disruption intensity), **surpriser** (low predictability, low disruption intensity), and **benign** (high predictability, low disruption intensity).

A catastrophic disruption is on most occasions difficult to predict in advance, often owing to it either being very infrequent or not having had a precedent. Along with this low predictability, which makes advance planning difficult, the high intensity of the disruption leads to severe damages to the supply chain, including the exit of businesses, as seen in the Ericsson example. Disruptions owing to severe weather, earthquakes, tsunamis, sudden government changes, or financial fraud are difficult to anticipate, while the disruption impact could be severe. Honda's assembly plant near Bangkok, among many other factories, was closed for over four months after the 2011 Thailand flooding, and many multinational firms evacuated from Libya after the 2011 civil war that deposed the Muammar Gaddafi government. Parmalat SpA, an Italian dairy multinational, fell victim to financial fraud, which led to the breakdown of its supply chain in 2003. The arrival of Apple iPhone and Android mobile phone operating systems contributed drastically to the collapse in demand for Nokia phones, resulting in severe long-term disruption to its supply chain. From 2007 to 2012, Nokia market capitalization fell from €110 billion to €14.8 billion.[7]

An anticipatable disruption, though of high disruption intensity, has the advantage of high predictability, which allows firms to be better prepared. For these disruptions, predictability is better owing to higher frequency of occurrence. For instance, Mumbai (India) receiving heavy rains during June to August is well known. These rains could flood its road and rail networks, bringing traffic to a standstill. Flights are also affected during heavy rains. However, the impact of heavy rains on Mumbai's industry is not huge, as firms can anticipate the disruptions in advance from experience. Similarly, most earthquakes or typhoons that hit Japan or the typhoons that hit China do not cause severe disruption to their supply chains, as firms have the experience of handling them in the past.

A surpriser disruption is like a catastrophic disruption with regard to predictability. However, unlike the catastrophic disruption, its immediate impact on the supply chain is lower. The 2018 tariff war between the USA and China was difficult to predict till its announcement. Though it would affect the financial calculations of various firms in different supply chains, it hasn't resulted in supply chain disruptions. Moderate currency swing is also a surpriser disruption, particularly when the supply chain in question criss-crosses multiple countries. Similarly, the sudden failure of a supplier with a good record, though disruptive, will be of limited impact if the buyer firm sources the material from multiple suppliers.

A benign disruption is the least harmful among different disruption types owing to high predictability and low disruption intensity. Heavy staff shortage during the holiday season in firms whose peak sales also occur at the same time, for instance retailers, could be disruptive. However, as its occurrence is known well in advance, firms can plan well such that the impact is minimal. Incidents like a country or a team winning a sports event (resulting in demand surge for some goods), an electricity outage, or an accident in the transport network can disrupt a supply chain. However, as these are regular phenomena that do not have a huge impact, firms are able to cope with them reasonably well.

From the preceding categorization of supply chain disruptions, we can argue that supply chain risk is high if the disruption is catastrophic. The supply chain risk is moderate for anticipatable or surpriser disruptions. Lastly, the supply chain risk is least for benign disruptions.

Measuring supply chain risk

Despite supply chain risk management assuming great significance, firms find it a challenge to measure and quantify the risks they face. A typical approach is to measure the probability of a risk based on past data and multiply that with the financial impact to obtain an expected estimate of the disruption. For instance, if the likelihood of extreme weather affecting a firm's supply chain is 10% and the consequent financial loss is $10 million, then the expected loss as a result of extreme weather is $1 million (10% of $10 million). Once the firm has studied the various sources of risk along with their likelihoods and potential damages, it can identify the sources that are riskiest along with the supply chain points that are most vulnerable. Based on the expected loss, the firm could make necessary investments to mitigate the concerned risk. While this description may sound very simple, firms face challenges on estimating the likelihoods as well as the financial impacts. A factory located on the seacoast may be vulnerable to a tsunami. However, if the probability of a tsunami at that site is once every 1000 years (hence, 0.1% likelihood of being struck in a particular year), the expected loss will turn out to be a miniscule number against the actual losses possible. The question would then be whether to factor this risk at all into the firm's calculations!

Holding inventory in the form of buffer stocks has been a strategy followed by firms for many supply chain risks. Measuring supply chain risk in such situations could be based on the number of days of buffer stock held. The higher the supply chain risk, the higher will be the number of days of buffer stock. This strategy works fine for all disruptions except the catastrophic ones. In the case of catastrophic disruptions, it may be wiser for the firm to have multiple arrangements instead of just one. It could imply multiple suppliers for the same material, multiple factories, or multiple modes of transport (discussed in detail in the next section). The additional cost incurred by the firm as a result of the multiple arrangements (including possible loss of scale economies) could be a measure of supply chain risk in such instances. Similarly, the premium charged by an insurance firm against a supply chain disruption is another measure of supply chain risk, whereby a high premium indicates high supply chain risk.

David Simchi-Levi of the Massachusetts Institute of Technology (MIT), along with two other academics, developed a method to help prioritize the financial or operational impact of risk. Their proposal estimates two measures – time to recovery (TTR) and time to survive (TTS). They define TTR as "the time it would take for a particular node – a supplier facility, a distribution center, or a transportation hub – to be restored to full functionality after a disruption" and TTS as the "maximum duration that the supply chain can match supply with demand after a node disruption." A particular site in the supply chain is exposed to risk when the TTS of the site is less than its TTR. While the authors recommend building inventory when TTS is lower than TTR, they also argue reduction of inventory when TTS is far greater than TTR.[8]

Supply chain risk management approaches

As discussed earlier, we could categorize the supply chain disruptions into four categories based on their predictability and disruption intensity. The risk management strategy to be adopted by a firm should be decided based on the disruption type. Brian Tomlin of the Tuck School of Business suggests financial mitigation, operational mitigation, and operational contingency as tactics for managing disruption risks. Financial mitigation refers to receiving compensation for disruptions by insuring against such risks. Operational mitigation in turn comprises inventory and sourcing tactics. While mitigation refers to action taken in advance of a disruption, contingency refers to action taken only when a disruption happens. The author describes operational contingency as comprising rerouting and demand management tactics.[9]

Financial mitigation

Financial mitigation through insurance coverage is a familiar tactic in managing supply chain disruptions. However, insurance compensation is only for the damages suffered by equipment, property, and material. It does not compensate for revenue or profits lost as a result of the disruption. At 2012 prices, the insured losses worldwide have increased steadily from less than $20 billion till 1988 to over $120 billion in 2011.[10] The higher losses lead to higher insurance premiums and, hence, a higher cost of doing business.

Operational mitigation through inventory

As already mentioned earlier, holding inventory in the buffer stock is another familiar tactic followed by firms in managing supply chain disruptions. For instance, the Central Electricity Authority of India prescribes the number of days of coal stock to be held by a power plant as a function of how far the plant is from the mine that supplies it coal. While the power plant may hold just 15 days' of stock if it is a pit-head station, the requirement increases to 30 days of stock if it is at least 1000 km away from the coal mine.[11] In this example, the distance between mine and plant is a proxy of supply chain disruption risk, the greater distance implying greater chance of disruption.

Operational mitigation through sourcing

From the viewpoint of rationalizing the supplier base as well as reducing overheads in procurement, the concept of single sourcing (only one supplier for a particular component or raw material) received strong impetus in the 1980s. The growing emphasis was to develop strategic relationships with the single suppliers who would jointly design the products they deliver instead of being restricted just to production only. A single supplier was fine if it had the ability to supply reliably from multiple production facilities. However, the increasing pressures to cut costs resulted in suppliers investing in a large plant instead of many smaller plants. Similarly, there have been trends in manufacturing too to concentrate production in fewer numbers of larger factories in place of a larger number of smaller factories to improve economies. The flip side of such approaches is the increased risk of supply chain disruption.

Imagine a firm daily procuring 1000 units of a raw material from a single supplier who carries a negligible buffer stock. A five-day disruption at this supplier end, apart from reducing the raw material supply by 5000 units, would also affect the output of the firm for those five days. Instead, imagine that the same firm daily procures 500 units each of the same material from two suppliers (dual sourcing). If each supplier has the ability to raise daily production by 50% (for instance through running an additional shift), the firm could still receive 750 units daily if there is a five-day disruption at the facility of one of the suppliers. In other words, the losses suffered by the firm by having two suppliers would only be 25% of what it would have suffered had it had only one supplier. The additional costs incurred as a result of having a second supplier should be evaluated, not against the procurement cost on that particular raw material, but against the disruption losses that the firm would suffer if it had only one supplier. Apple has been following a dual-sourcing strategy for its vital iPhone components. For instance, the component A9, a 64-bit ARM-based system-on-chip (SoC), is sourced from two suppliers, Samsung and TSMC. As each supplier would have a different process of designing and developing the component, the dual sourcing approach has resulted in two similar but not quite equal chips. Despite the cost of developing A9 becoming much higher, Apple went ahead with dual sourcing from the viewpoint of minimizing the risks of supply chain disruption as well as possible quality problems in the component.[12] The same article also points out that an IBM dual-sourcing requirement for x86 chips was the reason for supplier AMD to enter the x86 industry.

Like dual sourcing, another sourcing operational mitigation is to intentionally maintain some level of slack in production and to have a greater number of manufacturing locations. Firms like Toyota, Honda, and Nestlé are known for not fully utilizing their factory capacities so that the slack could be utilized when production at any of their plants is disrupted. Unlike the trends in recent times of concentrating manufacturing in a few locations, Nestlé has been expanding its manufacturing locations and has over 400 factories located in about 85 countries.

Operational contingency through rerouting

One of the best-known instances of operational contingency through rerouting is that of how the Toyota Group recovered after a fire halted the production at Aisin Seiki, the sole supplier of P-valves. Owing to following just-in-time (JIT) production, only two to three days' of stock was available, and the disruption was expected to affect the Toyota Group production for many weeks. However, through a collaborative effort involving over 200 firms, the production of P-valves was resumed quickly, and the various firms of the Toyota Group were back to normal activity one week after the disruption. The part drawings and machines required were shared with other suppliers of Toyota. Despite the absence of any prior experience of producing this component and the special purpose machines required for mass production, this group effort was able to restore the supply chain back to normalcy. The actual losses suffered by the different members of the Toyota supply chain turned out to be negligible compared to what was initially feared.[13]

Operational contingency through demand management

While operational contingency through rerouting describes the flexibility of a firm to quickly make changes to its supply chain, operation contingency through demand management describes the ability of a firm to alter its demand as a response to supply chain disruption. After an earthquake rocked Taiwan in 1999, the supply of certain semiconductors was affected. While many computer manufacturers were affected, Dell managed this episode by offering attractive pricing on computers whose production was not affected, thereby shifting the customer demand.[14] Chocolate manufacturers are known to promote demand for white chocolates or chocolates with lesser amounts of cocoa, through appropriate pricing and campaigns, whenever there is shortage of cocoa supply.

Risk management approaches for different disruption types

Table 7.1 describes the relevance of various risk management approaches for different disruption types. While disruption intensity is high for catastrophic and anticipatable disruptions, it is low for the other two. Hence, financial mitigation through costly insurance may not be warranted for such disruptions. Catastrophic and surpriser disruptions are very difficult to predict, and mitigating such disruptions through holding of inventory would be wasteful. It is prudent to invest in operational mitigation through sourcing and operational contingency through rerouting in such situations. Of course, operational contingency through rerouting is a prudent risk management approach even for anticipatable disruptions. An operational contingency through demand management may be necessary only for catastrophic disruptions, while it would be enough to just depend on operational mitigation through inventory for benign disruptions.

Table 7.1 Risk management (RM) approaches for various disruptions

RM approach	Catastrophic	Anticipatable	Surpriser	Benign
Financial mitigation through insurance	✓	✓		

Operational mitigation
   through inventory
   through sourcing
	
	✓
		
		✓
			
			✓
				
				✓

Operational contingency
   through rerouting
   through demand shifting
	
	✓
	✓
		
		✓
			
			✓	

Building supply chain resilience

Yossi Sheffi and James Rice of the Massachusetts Institute of Technology (MIT) argue that "building a resilient enterprise should be a *strategic initiative* that changes the way a company operates and that increases its competitiveness." They describe resilience as the ability to bounce back from a disruption, which can be achieved through either redundancy or increasing flexibility. They also argue that while redundancy is a perpetual cost with benefit only if there is a disruption, flexibility enables a firm to build competitive advantage in its operations.[14]

The Nestlé recovery after a test in India revealed traces of lead (beyond the permissible limit) and monosodium glutamate (not disclosed in the packaging) in Maggi Noodles, its bestselling product in India, speaks highly of its organizational flexibility and supply chain resilience. This finding in May 2015 led to a series of bans across several states in India, and Maggi sales plummeted. Before the crisis, Nestlé had a 77% market share of the Indian noodles market. Instead of challenging the ban or indulging in publicity campaigns, Nestlé withdrew the product and destroyed the stocks it had in hand. This act went a long way in building assurance in customer minds that Nestlé would not compromise on quality. In the following months, it was able to prove in India and abroad that the earlier revelation was a random case and that there was no serious quality issue. By November 2015, the Maggi Noodles sales resumed along with a safety campaign by Nestlé. Suresh Narayanan, who took over the reins of Nestlé India in October 2015, focussed on transparently communicating with all the stakeholders, suppliers, employees, distributors, and customers; the media; and FSSAI (Food Safety & Standards Authority of India).[15] By January 2017, the Maggi market share had crossed 60% and the firm had recaptured much of its lost market.

A warming planet is expected to contribute significantly to huge variations in climate in the years to come. Many studies indicate that instances of severe weather are expected to be more frequent as the earth gets warmer. There are also predictions that a warmer and globalized planet could see greater bouts of various epidemics like the Ebola and Zika virus outbreaks. There are also indications that after close to three decades of low barrier global trade, the world could see sporadic instances of policy interventions that could disrupt trade relations between countries. All this could imply that we are in no way near to a world free of supply chain disruptions. On the contrary, firms would have to be more alert and vigilant towards increasing vulnerability to various supply chain disruptions.

Strategic insights

- Excellent supply chains take a strategic rather than a reactive view to supply chain risk. The potential economic cost of disruption is factored in while designing the supply chain network.
- Excellent firms constantly monitor and measure supply chain risk. They plan their risk management approach in advance based on the perceived supply chain risk.
- There is increasing evidence to point to investment in supply chain resilience being critical to the long-term sustainability of a firm and its supply chains.

Notes

1 Mortimer, C. 2016. *Tianjin Explosion: Gigantic Crater Left by Chinese Factory Accident Revealed.* www.independent.co.uk/news/world/asia/tianjin-explosion-photos-china-chemical-factory-accident-crater-revealed-a7199591.html
2 www.dhl.com/content/dam/Campaigns/risk-and-resilience/dhl_insighton_final.pdf
3 Latour, A. 2001. *A Fire in Albuquerque Sparks Crisis for European Cell-Phone Giants.* www.wsj.com/articles/SB980720939804883010
4 Sickler, J. 2017. *Why a Great Company Reputation Is Important?* www.reputation management.com/blog/negative-company-reputation-affects-business/
5 Dsouza, S. 2018. *Patanjali's Sales Down First Time in Five Years.* www.bloombergquint.com/business/broken-supply-chain-drags-patanjalis-sales-down-first-time-in-five-years
6 Hendricks, K. B., & Singhal, V. R. 2003. The effect of supply chain glitches on shareholder wealth. *Journal of Operations Management,* 21(5), 501–522.
7 Shaughnessy, H. 2013. *Apple's Rise and Nokia's Fall Highlight Platform Strategy Essentials.* www.forbes.com/sites/haydnshaughnessy/2013/03/08/apples-rise-and-nokias-fall-highlight-platform-strategy-essentials/
8 Simchi-Levi, D. 2015. Find the weak link in your supply chain. *Harvard Business Review* (Digital Article). https://hbr. org/product/find-the-weak-link-in-your-supply-chain/H0242F-PDF-ENG

9 Tomlin, B. 2006. On the value of mitigation and contingency strategies for managing supply chain disruption risks. *Management Science*, 52(5), 639–657.

10 *Costly Calamities*. www.economist.com/graphic-detail/2013/03/27/costly-calamities

11 *New Methodology for Monitoring of Coal Stock at Coal Based Thermal Power Plants*. www.cea.nic.in/reports/others/planning/fm/guidelines_dcr.pdf

12 Smith, R. 2015. *Apple's A9 SoC is Dual Sourced from Samsung & TSMC*. www.anandtech.com/show/9665/apples-a9-soc-is-dual-sourced-from-samsung-tsmc

13 Nishiguchi, T., & Beaudet, A. 1998. The Toyota group and the Aisin fire. *MIT Sloan Management Review*, 40(1), 49–59.

14 Sheffi, Y., & Rice Jr, J. B. 2005. A supply chain view of the resilient enterprise. *MIT Sloan Management Review*, 47(1), 41–48.

15 *When It Comes to Putting Out Fires, Nestlé India's Suresh Narayanan Is No Novice*. www.forbes.com/sites/forbesasia/2018/01/17/when-it-comes-to-putting-out-fires-nestle-indias-suresh-narayanan-is-no-novice

8   Managing design for supply chain management

Various aspects of design have a strong bearing on supply chain performance. While the conventional design approach views product and process design primarily from the perspective of the consumer and the manufacturer, excellent supply chain management too has significant bearing on various design issues. We discuss these issues from the viewpoint of maximizing customer satisfaction while ensuring a high level of supply chain efficiency. The underlying assumption in this chapter is that, while customization has increased tremendously in recent times, a large chunk of goods consumed are still produced (at many stages of the production process if not all the stages) even before firms know precisely what individual customers are looking for. Hence, an important challenge for firms is to supply as close as possible to actual demand with minimal over- or under-production. Accordingly, managing the supply chain at a high velocity and "design for supply chain management" have assumed great significance.

Design for short product life cycles

Product life cycle describes the duration from product launch to product withdrawal in the primary market for which the product was designed. Marshall Fisher of Wharton School argues that products with long life cycles, which he describes as functional products, have stable and predictable demand. Typically, functional products face greater competition, which results in their having low profit margins. He describes short product life cycles as innovative products and argues that firms introduce innovative products as a means of increasing sales, pre-empting competition, and achieving higher profit margins. Garments, toys, mobile phones, and innovative food products are typical examples of day-to-day consumables that have short product life cycles. However, while an innovative product may have a higher profit margin, the newness in it results in its demand being unpredictable. Fisher recommends a responsive process for innovative products, which implies quick response, higher buffer capacity, lower lead time, and using modular product design.[2]

Firms that successfully manage short product life cycles have focussed both on design as well as the supply chain. With regard to design, modular product design has been a very popular approach among firms, particularly for products that have complex product structures like automobiles, computers, and mobile phones. Modular design ensures that a new product design does not mean all components have to be designed afresh. Another approach to design is "fast fashion" pioneered by Zara. Its new designs, based on the latest styles and trends, hit the stores in just a week or two, while the same could take close to six months for its competitors.[3]

To ensure that its quickly designed products reach showrooms immediately, Zara also pioneered a fast supply chain, which has already been described in Chapter 4. A fast supply chain that transacts in small batch sizes and short distances ensures that under- or over-supply of goods is minimal. Another supply chain initiative to manage short life cycle products is the speed factory pioneered by Adidas, which is a local production facility designed to quickly produce such products. The "Adidas Made for New York City" shoe (AM4NYC) is produced in a US speed factory instead of in Asia, which enables it to manage unpredictable demand much better.[4] The additional cost to business owing to a fast supply chain should be evaluated against the higher profits owing to fewer shortages and savings on lesser clearance sales.

Design for transportation, warehousing, and retailing

Many products that we consume are typically designed from the viewpoint of balancing the interests of the consumer against cost and other challenges in production. Different aspects of supply chain management, like transportation, storing, and retailing, have traditionally been accorded less importance in product design.

There are many examples of product or process designs not factoring transportation or storing issues. One such example is that of circular-shaped cookies being packed in cylindrical covers. This leaves empty space between the packets while they are arranged in cartons. As a result, carton space is not utilized fully and could even lead to product damage owing to rough handling. Unique product designs, while necessary to capture consumer interest, lead to challenges in packing and transport. As designs vary in physical dimensions, high product variety leads to high variety in packing material too. The packing material variety at an Indian tea packaging firm was so high that close to 90% of its Kolkata warehouse was used for storing packing material while less than 10% of the warehouse was used for holding tea. The reduced stocking of tea often resulted in the firm not being able to fully meet demand from its retailers. Similarly, an automobile battery manufacturer followed a production process of filling electrolyte and charging the battery at the factory itself, which meant heavier batteries being transported from the factory to the regional sales points. Owing to the presence of electrolyte in the battery, the trucks carrying batteries were under-utilizing the cargo space as they reached their maximum load in tonnes when only about 75% of the cargo space was filled. Had the electrolyte (an easily available material) filling and the battery charging been at the sales points, the per-truck dispatch from the factory could have been 30% more (hence, lower cost of transportation) while ensuring the energy discharge from the battery was minimal. The development of the square watermelon in Japan addressed some of the challenges in packing and transporting of the watermelons.[5] Another remarkable example of factoring the challenges in storing and transporting is that of ready-to-assemble furniture pioneered by IKEA. As assembly of the furniture is done only at the customer location, the firm is able to store and transport its products as flat-packs, which ensures that it can utilize its warehouse space and trucks far better than firms that sell pre-assembled furniture.[6]

Retailing too is affected by different aspects of product design and packing. There are many instances of packing which are appropriate from the viewpoint of visualization and attracting consumer attention but undesirable from the viewpoint of handling. For instance, instant noodle packets attract greater customer attention when stacked lengthwise on the retail shelf. However, this arrangement also carries a greater risk of the inventory falling from the shelf when a customer handles the product. To minimize potential damages to the product in handling, a retailer may arrange the material with the longer side pointing inwards, which would then hide the relevant portion of the packing from customer eyes. Similarly, retailer shelf designs may be such that manufacturers may not be able to use the space allotted optimally. The variation in retailer shelf designs could be a major reason for fast-moving consumer good (FMCG) pack size variations that are noticed for major retailers of the same product.

Facilities, logistics, and network design for fast supply chains

With the advent of quick and reliable tracking of material using technologies like bar-coding and RFID, the emphasis on faster flow of material has increased even further in modern supply chains. Reducing the number of transaction points in various stages of the supply chain has been an area of focus from the viewpoint of increasing the velocity of material flow.

Facilities design for fast supply chains

The famous Toyota Production System (TPS) includes practices like **direct delivery** of components without inspection to the assembly line and the supplier managing the component inventory at the Toyota assembly facility (**vendor managed inventory** or **VMI**). In many VMI systems, the buyer pays the vendor only for what has been consumed rather than for what has been delivered, which ensures that vendors do not stock more than what is required at the buyer facility. Indeed, the effort in recent times has been on investing in **flexible production** technologies (the speed factory of Adidas described earlier) that allow production in small batches. Rather than concentrating production in a few centres, as was the trend in the early 2000s, a rationale driven from the viewpoint of achieving a global scale of economies, firms are again focussing on the benefits of distributed production in increasing speed to market and decreasing supply chain risk. In 2018, Foxconn decided to set up LCD and TV assembly plants in the USA so that its products reach the market faster.[7] There is also an emphasis on locating facilities in or near clusters with greater availability of suppliers so that raw material is quickly available in situations of sudden demand surge.

Shipping solutions for fast supply chains

The need to reduce lead time and improve flow in global logistics has inspired many innovations. The standard 20- or 40-foot **intermodal container** is today the most popular means of transporting many types of finished goods. The container ensures that material once loaded at the producer factory need not be reorganized till it reaches the customer premises irrespective of how many ports it transits through. The container as the mode of carrying goods has facilitated innovations like **transhipment** and **multimodal transportation**. Almost 80% of the containers arriving at the Singapore port, one of the busiest in the world, are transhipped to other destinations in the world.[8] Containers arriving at the Rotterdam port can be shipped quickly to many destinations in Europe through multiple transport modes, including river barges, trains, or trucks. Railways in Europe and India offer the service of transporting goods-laden trucks on trains, which enables quicker and cleaner transportation. **Cross docking**, the direct transfer of consignments from one truck to another, is another time-saving practice that has gained ground in recent times. Thus, the design of many facilities in the supply chain, whether it is the factory, warehouse, or the shipment process, should facilitate quick movement of material with minimal transaction points.

Inbound and outbound logistics design for fast supply chains

Toyota was a pioneer in many benchmark inbound logistics practices too. Apart from Toyota City, whereby many suppliers located as close as possible to the Toyota plant, Toyota also practiced **milk run** and **component kitting**. **Milk run** referred to collecting supplies from various suppliers in one truck run so that the frequency of collecting material was very high. An exclusive truck to pick up material from a supplier would not allow frequent dispatches and would also increase the batch size. A milk run would be designed in such a way that a truck run would collect material from suppliers which are located close to each other. **Kitting** refers to picking up raw material in the same quantity from various vendors in the same truck run and bunching them as kits so that no time is wasted in sorting the material at the assembly line.

Similar innovations were pioneered by Dell in its outbound logistics. As Dell used to assemble only the CPU unit of the PCs it sold, the keyboard and monitor were not shipped to the Dell factory. Instead, the logistics firm would source them directly from the respective suppliers and **merge in transit** with the CPU unit in its journey to the end customer. The Asian Paints **delayed differentiation** example described in earlier chapters simplifies the outbound logistics to just the transportation of a few materials, namely base paints and pigments, which are converted into colour paints only at the retail outlet. This ensures that the lead time is short compared to what it would have been had the mixing been carried out at a central location like the factory. To improve the speed of doing business in the distribution part of the supply chain, many firms undertake packing and other customization activities at the final stages of the supply chain like retailing.

Network design for fast supply chains

As described in the beginning of this chapter, a great proportion of products sold worldwide even today follow the made to stock (MTS) system, which was described in Chapter 3. Production precedes customer ordering in an MTS system, which forces firms to forecast demand in advance of actual sales. As being highly efficient is a key objective of an MTS system, firms using the system naturally tend to give huge importance to capacity utilization in procurement, production, and transportation. This often is at the cost of supply chain velocity. Products or stock keeping units (SKUs) with low demand suffer more, as a quick supply chain would warrant production and transportation in small batches, which would result in loss of economies arising from transacting in large batches. Within a product line, after arranging the various SKUs in the descending order of sales, the top 20% of items that account for about 80% of total sales can be described as fast-moving SKUs. The remaining 80% of items that account for about 20% of the sales can be described as slow-moving SKUs. The supply chain network should be designed separately for fast-moving and slow-moving SKUs, as the same supply chain strategy for both SKUs would not be prudent.

We argue that demand of fast-moving SKUs would be more predictable than that of slow-moving SKUs owing to their demand volumes being higher. Because of the product being defined by standard features, fast-moving SKUs face greater competition and lower margins. Hence, it is imperative for fast-moving SKUs to compete on efficiency, while it is prudent to compete on responsiveness when it comes to slow-moving SKUs. In other words, while minimizing the total landed cost of the SKU at customer hands is appropriate for fast-moving SKUs, minimizing the lead time is appropriate for slow-moving SKUs. Given these objectives, the network design including aspects like batch quantity, where to procure from, where to locate production, where to stock finished goods, distribution planning, transport mode, and preferable retail channels are as described in Table 8.1. There are many instances in recent times where retailers are consciously following different networks for their fast-moving and slow-moving SKUs.

Another aspect of network design is about definition of sales territories. In many firms, the territories are often defined on extraneous factors like state boundaries rather than supply chain requirements. Hence, Pittsburgh in Pennsylvania would be supplied from a warehouse in Philadelphia rather

Table 8.1 Comparison of the supply chain network for fast-moving and slow-moving items

Detail	Fast-moving items	Slow-moving items
Demand (volume, predictability)	high, more predictable	low, less predictable
Product characteristics	standard features	customized features
Competition, profit margin	high, low	low, high
Demand forecasting	desirable	avoidable
Supply chain strategy	**efficiency**	**responsiveness**
Key performance measure	minimize total landed cost	minimize lead time
Batch quantity	large	small
Where to procure from	least cost suppliers	nearby suppliers
Production location	central	closer to customers
Finished goods stocking	closer to customers	at central locations
Distribution planning	made to stock (MTS)	made to order (MTO)
Transport mode	road, sea	air
Retail channel	stores as well as online	preferably online only

than Cleveland, which is the closer city. In India, where states are organized on linguistic basis, firms inadvertently define sales territories using state boundaries. As a result, it is common to see inefficient and criss-cross routing of material. In a consulting assignment carried out by one of the authors, the firm in question obtained material for its Gurgaon hub (very close to Delhi) from a Jalandhar warehouse and for its Ghaziabad and Agra hubs from a Lucknow warehouse (both hubs were closer to Delhi than Lucknow), while the Delhi warehouse served as a hub for a city as far away as Udaipur.

Design for reverse logistics and sustainability

Product and process design issues have assumed significant importance with the rise in product returns and reverse logistics. E-commerce growth and intense retail competition have led to liberal return policies adopted by both offline and online stores. This has given rise to increased consumer returns that have also impacted costs of processing and handling returns. The National Retail Federation in the USA, for example, estimated that close to $400 billion worth of merchandise was returned to retailers at the end of the 2018 holidays.[9]

Such a phenomenon has led to new challenges in handling product returns, transferring them back to the retailer's or third-party warehouses, or moving them back to the manufacturer's supply chain. In most cases, retailers resort to restocking the product if the condition of the returned product is as good as new or simply dispose of it – and many of these products reach landfills. However, increased focus on sustainability and emphasis on firms to be responsible for their products throughout their life cycles is changing this approach. Firms are investing in designing reverse logistics to move products back into their supply chains. Products can re-enter supply chains broadly under the following scenarios: when it's a *commercial return* as is the case of returns at retail stores, *end-of-use returns* when the customer returns a product like an obsolete-technology-based mobile phone in exchange for an advanced one, or *end-of-life returns* when the product has reached its end of life and has no further use.

Interestingly, in each of these scenarios, depending on the condition of the returned product, a decision has to be made on which route to undertake for managing such product returns. For example, if the commercial return can be brought back to as-good-as-new condition with minor repairs, then such activities can be carried out at the storefront itself. However, in other scenarios, firms have to establish testing facilities to decide the condition of the product, and depending on the condition of the returned "product-core," supply chain decisions are made. If the product core is in good condition, then a *refurbishment* can be carried out, and the product could be reintroduced back into the forward supply chain. In another circumstance, the product could be sent back to the manufacturer for *remanufacturing*. Lastly, if the product core and components of the returned product are not in usable condition, then such a product could be subjected to *recycling*.

Each of these stages in which a product re-enters the supply chain needs strategic focus. Several questions related to product returns arise – for example, are there bar codes or tags in returned products to match it to the batch sold by the manufacturer in the forward supply chain? Which player in the supply chain should collect and test the returned products? Should it be done by the retailer or the manufacturer or a third-party vendor? In designing reverse logistics too, firms face questions on economical ways to bring products back into supply chains. Unlike forward supply chains, where full-truckloads and efficient packaging methods can be deployed, the volume of returns may be uncertain. Further, returns can vary in sizes and shapes, making it difficult to devise efficient ways of transportation. Besides these, components and parts management of the returned products (in case of hi-tech products, white goods for example) are also challenging since firms have to trace and track the history of components manufactured in their production facilities. Despite these challenges, several firms, like HP, Cisco, and Caterpillar, have undertaken a keen interest in designing and implementing reverse supply chains and have benefitted from such investments.[10]

Distribution channels in the Internet era

The present decade has indeed been the "Amazon" decade with lots of consumer demand shifting from conventional store-based retailers (brick and mortar) to online retailers. While brick and mortar retailers grow at single digit rates annually, online retailing has been growing consistently at about 20% annually. Online retail sales now account for about 8.5% of total sales worldwide.[11] As the delivery of goods at customer homes shifts from customers to the retail firm, managing the supply chain in the e-commerce era is raising many new questions. Owing to online sales, the need to have multiple inventory points in the supply chain and huge stocks in the retail outlets is decreasing. While online retailing enables customers to reach to the actual manufacturers quickly through platforms like Amazon and Alibaba, the last mile of delivery is increasingly turning out to be challenging. Home deliveries suffer from poor economies, particularly if the customers are located far away from the online retailer's distribution point. In many parts of the world, there is a shortage of labour for delivery activities, compelling online firms to explore other means of delivery. While delivery of consignments through drones is still a few years away (JD of China is already using drones in certain routes),[12] retailers are experimenting with "click and collect" models, whereby customers collect their consignments from retailers' collection points. Many conventional retailers are moving to become hybrid retailers with the utility of the physical store shifting from being a stocking point to one where customers could try various exhibited samples and order the product they like, which would be delivered at home. While certain industries like personal computers have witnessed e-commerce enabling the ultimate form of customization, whereby the customer designs the product he or she purchases, such sales continue to be a negligible share of total retail sales. Online retailing in conjunction with various innovations in the last mile is expected to break the final frontier of effectiveness.

Strategic insights

- An "efficiency only" slow-moving supply chain is least appropriate for short life cycle products in today's fast environment.
- Various factors in packaging, transportation, warehousing, and retailing have a strong bearing on how well a product is perceived by its retail customers and how well its supply chain is managed. Incorporating these factors in product design is a characteristic of excellent supply chains.
- Excellent firms take an integrative and attention-to-details approach to design and are at the forefront of investing in fast supply chains. They are also leaders in design for reverse logistics and sustainability.

Notes

1 Kuiti, M. R., Ghosh, D., Gouda, S., Swami, S., & Shankar, R. 2019. Integrated product design, shelf-space allocation and transportation decisions in green supply chains. *International Journal of Production Research*, 1–21.
2 Fisher, M. L. 1997. What is the right supply chain for your product? *Harvard Business Review*, 75, 105–117.
3 *The Secret of Zara's Success: A Culture of Customer Co-creation.* https://martinroll.com/resources/articles/strategy/the-secret-of-zaras-success-a-culture-of-customer-co-creation/
4 *How "Speed Factories" Help Companies Adapt to Capricious Consumers.* https://insight.kellogg.northwestern.edu/article/how-speed-factories-help-companies-adapt-to-capricious-consumers
5 *Square Fruit Stuns Japanese Shoppers.* http://news.bbc.co.uk/2/hi/asia-pacific/1390088.stm
6 Brownlee, J. 2016. *The Man Behind Ikea's World-Conquering Flat-Pack Design.* www.fastcompany.com/3057837/the-man-behind-ikeas-world-conquering-flat-pack-design
7 *Trump Hails Foxconn Breaking Ground on $10bn US Plant.* https://asia.nikkei.com/Economy/Trade-War/Trump-hails-Foxconn-breaking-ground-on-10bn-US-plant

8 *Why Malaysian Ports Are Losing Out to Singapore.* www.todayonline.com/world/why-malaysian-ports-are-losing-out-singapore

9 Ladd, B. 2018. *The Retail Industry Has a Problem with Returns: ReturnRunners Wants to be the Solution.* www.forbes.com/sites/brittainladd/2018/12/19/retailers-are-about-to-get-hit-with-95b-of-holiday-returns-returnrunners-can-recover-those-losses/#3f2d81c826b6

10 Jayaraman, V., & Luo, Y. 2007. Creating competitive advantages through new value creation: A reverse logistics perspective. *Academy of Management Perspectives*, 21(2), 56–73.

11 *E-commerce Takes Off.* www.economist.com/special-report/2017/10/26/e-commerce-takes-off

12 *Logistics Need a Shake-up.* www.economist.com/special-report/2017/10/26/logistics-need-a-shake-up

9   Green and sustainable supply chains

In 2015, the United Nations chartered 17 sustainable development goals that were adopted by several countries. Some of these goals pertain to affordable and clean energy, clean water, sanitation, climate change, and responsible production and consumption.[2] While several of these goals create an onus on governments to develop suitable policies and regulatory ecosystems to achieve these targets, there are far-reaching implications for businesses too. In particular, with widening ecological footprints of supply chains (where a shirt stitched in Bangladesh is sold in a store in the USA or a phone assembled in Taiwan is sold in a store in the UK), firms are finding it increasingly difficult to manage complex product flows through the network of multi-tiered suppliers, contract manufacturers, logistics partners, truckers, and shippers. With sourcing of products spanning multiple geographies, the environmental impact of production, transportation, and packaging processes have significantly increased. This has also led to an increase in the risk of environmental or social damage owing to supply chain activities that are either not monitored or are ignored. However, frequently occurring day-to-day supply chain issues often become the priority of managers, leaving environmental or social issues pertaining to supply chain activities to be neglected. Under these circumstances, the pertinent question remains whether managers need to prioritize sustainable supply chain issues over economic goals. The answer lies in observing certain events and drawing lessons from them.

BP, one of the world's largest oil and gas companies, was found responsible for an oil spill in the Gulf of Mexico in the southern coast of the USA in 2010 which led to the deaths of 11 workers and approximately 134 million gallons of oil spilled in the waters of the Gulf of Mexico.[3] Also called the *Deepwater Horizon* oil spill, the event led to severe loss of fishing and business activities across the coastal areas of Mississippi, Louisiana, and Alabama, in addition to significant loss of marine life, and was termed the biggest environmental disaster in US history. The expenses related to preventing oil leakage and settling litigations as an aftermath of this environmental disaster cost BP more than $65 billion, along with then CEO of BP Tony Hayward being asked to step down.[4]

In a different industry, in 2007, Mattel, one of the world's largest toy makers, was forced to recall close to 19 million toys from retail shelves when it was found that several of these toys had impermissible levels of lead paints that were harmful for kids. In addition, several toys also had tiny magnets that could be easily swallowed. Much of Mattel's toys were primarily manufactured and assembled in China, and despite close ties and long-term relations with China-based suppliers, it was found that several of their contract manufacturers and paint suppliers had flouted norms.[5] The outcome of the series of toy recalls was not only felt on the retailer's shelves with the loss of sales and erosion of trust on the brand, but also on the supplier side with China banning several of these suppliers and implementing stricter norms. Not only did Mattel invest in costly toy recalls, it also had to commit to costly monitoring of its China-based production facilities. In addition, Mattel ran full-page advertisements in leading newspapers to convince customers to return to its products.[6]

In another example, in the 1990s, Nike, one of the world's largest designer and manufacturers of athletic footwear and apparel, faced a significant challenge arising out of its geographically spread supply chains. With the growth of outsourcing in the 1990s, Nike had spread its manufacturing facilities to several low-cost regions, such as Indonesia, Cambodia, China, Pakistan, and Vietnam. But closer media scrutiny of the production facilities in these regions revealed that much of the labour involved in stitching Nike soccer balls and apparel was child labour. Further, Nike was also criticized for sourcing products from such production facilities where low wages, poor working conditions, and human rights abuses were rampant. Such information significantly affected the brand image of the firm, and many customers, in particular, college students, refused to purchase Nike products.[7] The loss of sales and erosion of trust compelled Nike to undertake significant steps over the course of several years with costly investments in closely monitoring its suppliers, working with them in maintaining wage standards and suitable working conditions, and committing to reduce waste, toxins, and CO_2 emissions from its supply chains.

What lessons can be drawn from these examples? With globally spread supply chains, firms cannot ignore the environmental and social impact of activities within their supply chains. In addition, negative environmental and social externalities have the potential to impact financial performance of firms significantly. Specifically, firms with large environmental and social footprints also stand a higher risk of scrutiny from media, customers, regulatory authorities, and non-governmental organizations, and ignoring the social and environmental impact of supply chains can lead to significant loss of sales, lack of trust, and brand value erosion. In other words, economic goals cannot be viewed in isolation from environmental and social goals. Thus, it is imperative to incorporate sustainability values in supply chains and operations. This brings forth an important question, namely, what factors drive sustainability initiatives of firms?

The United Nations defines sustainable development as "development that meets the need of the present without compromising the ability of future generations to meet their own needs."[8] Three elements that are critical to achieving this objective are *economic growth*, *social inclusion*, and *environmental protection*.[8] While these elements are objectives for governments and societies, for firms and supply chains as well, this has led to the emergence of what is called the *triple bottom line approach*.[9] The triple bottom line framework suggests that firms should define environmental and social goals along with economic objectives and work towards them. The triple bottom line framework sets a difficult yet achievable task for firms to consider environmental and social aspects in their operations and supply chains in addition to economic objectives. So how can firms achieve these goals?

Factors that drive sustainability (environmental) initiatives in organizations

Conceptually, the simple profit equation of a firm given by profit = (price – unit cost) × sales quantity drives several managerial lessons. *Ceteris paribus*, each factor in the profit equation highlights the role that decision makers can play. Observe that price, unit cost, and sales quantity are three levers that impact the profit of a firm. The potential to charge a higher price, unit cost reduction, and an increase in sales quantity can drive higher profits. In other words, if sustainability initiatives can increase the ability of firms to charge higher prices (also called the *price premium* effect), reduce unit costs (also called the *cost reduction* effect), or increase sales quantity (also called the *demand expansion* effect), then such initiatives provide economic incentives for supply chain managers to undertake sustainability initiatives.[10]

To illustrate this further, consider the organic food and clothing industry. In India, for example, this industry is estimated to grow to a potential value of $1.36 billion by 2020 with a year on year growth rate of 20%.[11] Much of the organic food and clothing sold through retail stores is sold at a higher price point than normal goods. Similar observation applies to the electrical and electronics industry, where products with energy efficiency ratings and LED bulbs have replaced many of the shelves containing incandescent bulbs. Several of these product innovations are priced higher than equivalent non-green (or brown) products. However, companies continue to invest in these products since the potential to charge higher prices for several of these products drives economic profitability.

A similar argument holds for the demand expansion effect of sustainability (specifically environmentally friendly initiatives). A demand expansion effect means that the potential market for a product increases with the increase in its greening value. In other words, given a choice between two competing products with similar features, the consumer prefers the one which is more environmentally friendly. The demand expansion effect can be observed in the case of the automotive industry, where rising concerns over fuel emissions and costs have led to several innovations by Toyota, Tesla, Ford, and Volvo, among others, to introduce variants of fuel-efficient cars and electric vehicles.[12]

Growing concerns of consumers over the quality of food products and water has also led to the entry of consumer goods companies in this space. The availability of safe drinking water for millions of households in an emerging economy like India is a challenge. This also presents an opportunity for firms to develop and position products which cater to the growing consumer needs while being environmentally friendly. Thus, companies like Tata Chemicals[13] and Hindustan Unilever (HUL)[14] have created innovations like water purifiers named *Tata Swach*[15] and *Pureit*,[16] respectively, which are portable, do not require separate energy to run the product, and provide quality drinking water to households. In addition to this, in alignment with Unilever's Sustainable Living Plan,[17] the company has come up with innovations in shampoos, washing detergents, and so on which require less water during production as well as consumer use. Complex issues pertaining to environment and communities, particularly in emerging economies, provide organizations with an opportunity to innovate in supply chains to offer products and change processes that have the potential to expand markets and increase profitability.

The cost reduction potential bearing sustainability goals is inherent to any cost reduction objectives that supply chain managers aim to achieve. Fundamentally, an increase in efficiency of processes does naturally mean less environmental waste. For industry sectors such as apparel, fashion, plastic, and chemical manufacturing, for example, higher process efficiency, energy saving, technological innovations, and less material wastage are often objectives of cost reduction projects.[18] Thus, achieving environmental objectives are inherent in cost reduction objectives. A key focus area for cost reduction projects for supply chain partners has been the area of packaging. Both retailer and consumer packaged goods companies have collaborated to reduce packaging of products. Unilever, for example, introduced a reduced size of its "all small and mighty" detergent bottle in response to Walmart's policy change of selling only concentrated liquid laundry detergent at its discount stores in 2007.[19] Similar initiatives have also been taken in other product categories, such as deodorants, where Unilever reduced the pack-size of deodorant offerings, which would reduce the environmental impact of aerosols, while simultaneously offering the same number of sprays in a compressed deodorant.[20]

However, from a supply chain perspective, cost reduction projects (or sustainability projects) can lead to conflicting objectives between supply chain partners in certain cases. For example, a paint consumption reduction program run by an automotive manufacturer can directly impact the sales of its paints supplier. While the manufacturer would aim to run the program as a cost reduction measure or an environmental and health friendly initiative (since chemicals used in paints are often deemed harmful for health and environment with continuous usage), any reduction in paint volumes would mean a direct reduction in sales for the paint supplier. In such a case, suitable incentives or mechanisms need to be designed such that both partners benefit while collaborating in the paint reduction program. A discussion on how incentives of supply chain partners can be aligned is in Chapter 5.

It is thus clear that with potential economic benefits, firms can undertake sustainability initiatives in supply chains. However, economic factors may not be the only drivers of sustainability initiatives.

The role of regulations

A critical factor which often shapes the competitive strategy of firms and also plays an important role in supply chain decision making is government policy. Regulations such as carbon (or environmental) tax, cap-and-trade policies, and waste and emissions regulations have significant potential to impact supply chains. For example, the Restriction on Hazardous Substances (RoHS) and Waste Electrical and Electronic Equipment (WEEE) legislations,[21] first implemented in Europe, produced significant challenges for manufacturing firms and their supply chain partners. The legislations meant that firms had to be responsible for the entire life cycle of the products and prevent products from entering landfills, besides having to obey restrictions on the quality of chemicals and materials being used to manufacture products. The impact of such regulations can alter the competitive strategy of firms. The WEEE legislations, for example, meant that manufacturers had to redesign products with a longer life cycle and invest in the quality of materials being used in manufacturing products for longer durability and with properties of recyclability. It also meant that electrical and electronic equipment manufacturers had to rethink ways of collecting products after they had reached their end of life or end of use.

Challenges related to product collection pertain to ways of incentivizing customers to return products, establishing collection centres, investing in testing equipment and personnel at the collection points, and establishing reverse logistics to bring back products into production centres depending on the type of processing required. Processing type could be repairs, refurbishing, or recycling, depending on the quality of the product core that is returned. It is intuitively obvious that while forward supply chains pose several challenges in managing products, reverse logistics adds additional complexity of product collection, warehousing, inventory management, and recycling.

In addition to these, there are strategic issues that manufacturing firms face. For example, which distribution channel should they use to sell the refurbished products? Considering that price points of refurbished or recycled products are often less than the new products, how do they make sure that customers looking for new products do not buy refurbished products (with similar quality features) because of the price differential? Other issues pertain to the brand value of the manufacturing firms. Do refurbished or recycled products diminish the brand value of firms? Or do they increase it for environmentally conscious consumers? Further, firms may not have capacities to invest in reverse logistics and remanufacturing, in which case, they prefer to outsource the activities to a third-party firm. However, risks related to theft of intellectual property and loss of brand value and products arise with such arrangements. These issues become particularly acute in emerging economies where intellectual property and secondary markets are not strictly monitored. Several of these challenges are still being resolved and do not have easy answers.

Pollution regulations also have quite evident impact on the automotive industry, where stringent pollution norms that have come into effect globally have forced manufacturers to innovatively redesign both commercial and passenger vehicles. The automotive industry has been at the forefront of innovation vehicle design and has experimented with fuel cells, hybrid versions, and electrical vehicles, all with the aim to design products to reduce environmental pollution and adhere to changing government norms.

It can be argued that once government norms come into force, they can significantly alter firm behaviour. Those firms which have proactively invested in pollution, waste, and emissions control, technology, and products stand to benefit significantly from those which have not. The result may be the imposition of severe financial penalties on industry laggards. For example, strict emission standards globally forced one of the top European vehicle manufacturers to falsely report its vehicle emissions, leading to significant penalties and litigations thereafter.[22]

Green supply chain management

So what does green supply chain management entail? A green supply chain is defined as "Integrating environmental thinking into supply chain management including product design, material sourcing and selection, manufacturing processes, delivery of the final product to the consumers as well as end-of-life management of the product after its useful life."[23] Broadly, there are a few key metrics that are measured as a part of green supply chain management, namely, energy consumption, water consumption, greenhouse gas emission, and waste generation. Since it is a supply-chain-centric view, the impact of these metrics must cover all the activities in the supply chain that are required to extract raw materials, convert them into final products, and deliver them to the final consumer. Needless to say, such measurement requires the concerted effort of supply chain entities to measure and report metrics. Importantly, the measurement must also consider the metrics at the consumer usage stage and post-consumer use till the good either enters back into the supply chain or enters the landfill. Such measurement efforts are often time-consuming and costly. However, several firms have made a determined effort to measure the impact of their supply chain activities in the forward supply chain.

One such firm is Patagonia,[24] a designer for outdoor clothing and gear, based in the USA, which launched a program called "The Footprint Chronicles." As a part of the program, the firm has increased transparency and traceability in its supply chain by developing a tool to showcase the presence of globally spread farms, textile mills, and factories in its supply chain. For each of those supply chain members, the firm tracks the flow of material and the environmental impact of its operations up to its warehouses. Further, a customer looking up a product on Patagonia's website can click on the details to understand the design and material used, the origins of the material, and its impact on the environment. For several of its products, Patagonia reports the key metrics of its product flows, namely, the energy and water consumed, related greenhouse gas emissions, and waste generation, if any. Interestingly and contrary to popular belief, the company remains highly growth driven and an innovative company in the apparel industry.

The social aspect of sustainability

One of the key aspects of sustainability is the welfare of people. This involves better working conditions for workers, protection of workers' health and safety, better payroll schemes, increase in employee diversity, and support of local communities, among others. Firms which have ignored the social aspects of supply chains have experienced financial losses or closure of operations in markets where workers or communities have been adversely affected. One such case is a series of Bangladesh factory fires which led to the deaths of hundreds of workers between the years 2003–2015.[25] Investigations revealed that most of these factories operated in unsafe working conditions and catered to top apparel retail companies in the USA and Europe. The fires and loss of human lives created pressure on the apparel companies to jointly commit towards providing safer working conditions for the employees in the outsourced factories, provide better wages, and closely monitor the suppliers' performance in protecting human lives.

Social welfare as an objective of sustainable operations (similar to environmental goals) has consequences on the financial performance of firms. A case in point is Indian conglomerate ITC,[26] which has successfully integrated social welfare with economic objectives. ITC's well-studied *e-choupal*[27] initiative is a model of direct procurement through Internet-driven kiosks established in rural villages of India. While this model of direct procurement can be looked at from various lenses, the social welfare perspective aptly justifies the win-win model designed by ITC, where farmers receive regular information on crop prices, farming practices, and so on and support through kiosks while in return ITC procures high-quality fresh produce, experiencing stability in supply and prices. The model sustains both the firm and the communities in which it operates while driving economic rewards.

Sustainability goals have a key role to play in supply chain design and operations and will assume critical importance with rising issues in climate change. There are growing calls for firms to move away from a shareholder perspective to a stakeholder perspective to include employees, consumers, the environment, and communities' views, which also play an important role in the economic growth of firms.[28] Indeed, there are challenges of adapting sustainable goals since immediate benefits are often difficult to quantify, and, in several cases, there are trade-offs between economic objectives and sustainability goals. The Pareto efficient firms, however, are those which successfully design supply chains balancing these trade-offs.

Strategic insights

- Firms are under the increasing scrutiny of stakeholders, such as consumers, policy-making bodies, NGOs, and local communities considering the environmental and social impact of products and processes.
- Factors such as market demand expansion, price premium, and cost reduction effects can serve as important drivers of green initiatives.
- Wherever voluntary actions of firms have failed to adequately drive green initiatives, policy changes and regulations have played an important role in influencing such initiatives. Policy changes can alter the

competitive landscape of a firm and render significant disadvantage to polluting firms.

• Social good and community welfare are the additional aspects of sustainability initiatives of firms.

Notes

1 *Indian Officials Order Coco-Cola Plant to Close for Using Too Much Water.* www.theguardian.com/environ ment/2014/jun/18/indian-officals-coca-cola-plant-water-mehdiganj

2 *The Sustainable Development Agenda.* www.un.org/sustainabledevelopment/development-agenda/

3 *BP Oil Spill: Judge Grants Final Approval for $20bn Settlement.* www.theguardian.com/environment/2016/apr/04/bp-oil-spill-judge-grants-final-approval-20-billion-dollar-settlement

4 *BP's Deepwater Horizon Bill Tops $65bn.* www.theguardian.com/business/2018/jan/16/bps-deepwater-horizon-bill-tops-65bn

5 *Mattel Recalls 19 Million Toys Sent from China.* www.nytimes.com/2007/08/15/business/worldbusiness/15imports.html

6 *Unsafe for Children: Mattel's Toy Recalls and Supply Chain Management.* www.gsb.stanford.edu/faculty-research/case-studies/unsafe-children-mattels-toy-recalls-supply-chain-management

7 *How Nike Solved Its Sweatshop Problem.* www.businessinsider.com/how-nike-solved-its-sweatshop-problem-2013-5

8 *The Sustainable Development Agenda.* www.un.org/sustainabledevelopment/development-agenda/

9 *Triple Bottom Line.* www.economist.com/news/2009/11/17/triple-bottom-line

10 We discuss sustainability here primarily from an environmental (or greening) perspective. We discuss the social dimension of sustainability in a later section.

11 *Organic Food Market growing at 25–30%, Awareness Still Low: Govt.* https://timesofindia.indiatimes.com/business/india-business/Organic-food-market-growing-at-25-30-awareness-still-low-Govt/articleshow/49379386.cms

12 https://home.kpmg.com/xx/en/home/insights/2015/12/kpmg-global-automotive-executive-survey-2016.html

13 Tata Chemicals is a subsidiary of Tata Group with significant operations in India and Africa (www.tatachemicals.com/About-Us/Company-profile).

14 Hindustan Unilever (HUL) is the Indian subsidiary of consumer goods company Unilever, with headquarters in Mumbai, India (www.hul.co.in/).

15 www.tatachemicals.com/Asia/Products/Consumer-products/Water-purifiers/Tata-Swach-non-electric-water-purifier

16 www.pureitwater.com/IN/

17 *Sustainable Living.* www.hul.co.in/sustainable-living/the-unilever-sustainable-living-plan/

18 In certain cases, technology innovations may be costly in the short term but provide cost benefits in the long run.

19 Lai, K. H., Cheng, T. C. E., & Tang, A. K. 2010. Green retailing: factors for success. *California Management Review*, 52(2), 6–31.

20 www.compresseddeodorants.com/

21 http://ec.europa.eu/environment/waste/

22 *Dieselgate Scandal: What Options Does Volkswagen Have to Get Out of this Mess?*www.forbes.com/sites/sarwantsingh/2015/11/25/dieselgate-scandal-what-options-does-volkswagen-have-to-get-out-of-this-mess
23 Srivastava, S. K. 2007. Green supply-chain management: A state-of-the-art literature review. *International Journal of management Reviews*, 9(1), 53–80.
24 www.patagonia.com/footprint.html
25 *Bangladesh Textile Factory Fire Leaves More than 100 Dead.* www.theguardian.com/world/2012/nov/25/bangladesh-textile-factory-fire
26 ITC is a large Indian conglomerate diversified into various business lines with net revenues of $8 billion (www.forbes.com/companies/itc/#6a581b696a89).
27 www.itcportal.com/businesses/agri-business/e-choupal.aspx
28 Sodhi, M. S. 2015. Conceptualizing social responsibility in operations via stakeholder resource-based view. *Production and Operations Management*, 24(9), 1375–1389.

10 Popular supply chain analytics

In Chapter 1, we defined supply chain management as *efficient and effective coordination of material and information flows among suppliers, manufacturers, distributors, and customers so that a wide variety of products could be delivered quickly while keeping costs as low as possible.* The subsequent chapters dealt with various aspects of supply chain management. A common thread in all these chapters and the aspect that makes supply chain coordination so challenging is the uncertainties faced by the supply chain. Supply chain analytics has in recent times assumed great significance as a means of diagnosing various supply chain uncertainties and in devising solutions for the various challenges faced. The 2018 Gartner survey of the top 25 supply chain firms highlights the role supply chain analytics is playing in the pursuit of excellence. Some of the valuable supply chain analytics that should be carried out by firms are described in this chapter.

Basic statistics

At the broad level, data analyzed could be categorized into two broad areas. The first category is where the objective of analysis is to crunch the data minutely to get the breakup as granular as possible. The unit of analysis is typically in percentage terms. Examples include (i) sales breakup region-wise, retailer format-wise, or product-wise; (ii) classification of items as fast moving or slow moving; and (iii) procurement breakup region-wise, vendor-wise, and so on. Variability is not a focus in this analysis category.

The second category is where the objective of analysis is not just to understand the data breakup but also to understand the variability of the data being studied. Production, dispatch, sales, inventory, and lead time are typical examples of data studied where just measuring the average alone is insufficient, and better decision making is dependent on proper understanding of the variability. In such analysis, apart from mean or median, the firm would also take efforts to determine standard deviation (measure of variability).

Table 10.1 Time taken by a logistics firm to delivers goods to a retailer

Consignment	1	2	3	4	5	6	7	8	9	10	11	12	13	14	15	16	17	18	19	20	Average
Number of days	5	3	4	3	3	2	5	4	2	4	3	2	4	5	4	5	4	2	3	3	3.5

The Table 10.1 indicates the delivery history of a logistics provider who delivers goods to a retailer. Based on data available for 20 deliveries, it can be seen that the average of delivery days is 3.5 days. Further analysis shows that the delivery days taken were either two days (four instances or 20%), three days (six instances or 30%), four days (six instances or 30%), and five days (four instances or 20%). This is known as the estimation of the probability distribution, which is an essential step in the analysis of variability. Based on these data, we can conclude that there is a 100% chance that lead time is at least two days, an 80% chance that lead time is at least three days, and a 50% chance that lead time is at least four days. Like this, a supply chain manager can collect various types of supply chain data and understand the variability observed in the data concerned.

Predicting scenarios

In the data analyzed earlier, let us describe a lead time of less than 3.5 days (average lead time) as early delivery and a lead time greater than 3.5 days as delayed delivery. This implies two scenarios for retailer orders of 50% each as far as delivery lead time is concerned. Let the retailer order be either low (50 units with a 40% probability) or high (100 units with a 60% probability). Thus, the combination of delivery lead time and retailer order can create four scenarios: early delivery – low demand ($0.5 \times 0.4 = 20\%$ probability); early delivery – high demand (30% probability); late delivery – low demand (20% probability); and late delivery – high demand (30% probability).

Supply chain managers can, based on the data they handle, create many decision scenarios using past data. The probabilities and corresponding intensities of the issue in hand can thus be estimated using past data. Past data are a very good indicator of potential scenarios that would be faced by the supply chain. Hence, a supply chain manager can estimate in advance the possibility of undesirable scenarios as well as desirable scenarios.

Demand analytics and the hockey stick effect

In many firms, the analysis of demand is typically on a monthly basis. The analysis of demand at a broader time unit like the month or quarter hides the various discrepancies that can be noticed only if the unit of time is a week or a day. Seasonal behaviours like higher sales in the last week of the month or on specific days of a week get noticed only when we analyze data at a more granular level. The bullwhip effect described in Chapter 5 could be noticed only after retail demand was analyzed at a granular level. Such a granular-level analysis revealed that the order fluctuation noticed at the factory level was not observed at the retail level.

Another such discrepancy noticed widely in many supply chains is the end of the month sales peaking as a result of monthly sales targets. In a wide variety of industries that still operate on the made-to-stock basis with monthly sales targets, the initial weeks of the month report very few sales. However, as managers get closer to the end of the month, the sales machinery shifts to the faster lane. This sales peak at the end of the month is described in many industries as the hockey stick effect. The hockey stick effect is a source of inefficiency in supply chains. It results in mismatches between supply and demand at different stages of the supply chain. The mismatches are often managed by carrying high levels of inventory particularly closer to the retail points. The higher the hockey stick effect, the larger would be the warehousing requirement, as the inventory built in the distribution channel is inactive for a considerable part of the month.

Apart from analyzing demand data at shorter time intervals, like the day or week, analysis of demand at the SKU level is far more informative than analyzing demand at the aggregate level. It is possible to observe discrepancies in demand between fast-moving and slow-moving SKUs or shortages and excesses in stocks only if the unit of analysis is the SKU. Similarly, the customer service level and fill rate analysis should be carried out at the SKU level and at shorter time intervals if a firm wishes to understand how effective its supply chain is. Such exercises carried out at an aggregate level and at time intervals like the month would only result in many of the discrepancies being hidden.

Inventory and lost sales analytics

Inventory is a commonly conducted data-based analysis in supply chain management. As described in Chapter 2, the closing stock of a given day is the opening stock of that day plus the net material inflow (inflow minus the outflow). We also discussed that once we have the closing (or opening) stock of all the days, we can determine the average closing (or opening) stock held at that inventory point. By dividing the average inventory by the daily production, dispatch, or sales rate at the inventory point, we can easily describe average inventory in terms of number of days. For instance, if the production rate of an item is 100 units a day and if the average inventory of that item at the production point is 350 units, then we can say that the average inventory of that item is equivalent to 3.5 days at this production point.

Inventory statistics are readily available in an ERP database. However, it may also be kept in mind that for firms with a large material list and many levels of inventory, recording the inventory data at a granular level (say daily and at SKU level) could be very challenging. Given the ease of computing of inventory, it may be kept in mind that storing inventory data need not be an important consideration while designing the firm's information systems. Instead, the ability to quickly retrieve the information required for calculating inventory at the granular level should receive greater consideration.

Measuring lost sales is more challenging than measuring inventory, particularly given the intangibility associated with it. However, not measuring lost sales often leads to conservative inventory decisions, which in turn result in the firm falling short on its sales potential. Observing the number of occasions of zero inventory and the duration of time the inventory point is stocked-out (zero inventory level) is a means of understanding lost sales at the simplest level. If the inventory point is in the control of another firm (say a retail point of an FMCG manufacturer), the information sharing between the firms should incorporate means of measuring stock-outs and stock-out durations. This is much easier in business-to-business (B2B) transactions, as they are increasingly automated. However, it is still not a common phenomenon that supplier firms entirely capture the sales that they fail to meet. Part of the problem is owing to lost sales statistics not receiving the importance they deserve. Firms with greater customer focus have typically been ahead of industry when it comes to capturing lost sales information and analyzing the same.

Lead-time analytics

Earlier chapters have emphasized the importance of firms and supply chains competing on shorter lead times. However, the greatest hurdle to this objective is the difficulty firms face in measuring and analyzing their lead times. Apart from minimizing lead times, it is also important for firms to have reliable and consistent lead times. High lead-time variation is not a sign of a healthy supply chain.

For instance, interaction with supply chain managers of an Indian firm revealed that the managers perceived the firm's supply chain (from factory to material being handed over to its retailers) to be of one-month duration only. However, a detailed lead-time analysis pointed out that the total time spent as inventory at various stages of the supply chain along with the time spent in transit between the various stages easily added to more than three months. Sample analysis at retail outlets of the manufacturing date mentioned on its products also confirmed that the products were more than three months old when they were purchased by the end customers. This situation is owing to lead-time analysis not receiving enough attention among supply chain managers and often to managers not employing easily available technological solutions.

In the era of most products being barcoded or carrying RFID tags, recording lead time is technically not a difficult task. While we notice that firms do capture lead-time statistics of individual segments of the supply chain, many firms do not accord sufficient importance to measuring the same on an end-to-end basis (i.e., from sourcing to retailing). In another instance, it was noticed that the ERP software in a firm had provisions to capture the starting and ending time of each stage of its overall production process. Despite the availability of data, it was observed that the firm had no clue about the overall supply chain lead time of the products it produced, as the required queries and reports had not been created in its information systems.

Where the firm does not have the ability to collect the start and finish times of each unit processed at different stages owing to production being in big lots or batches, an approximate lead-time analysis could be carried out by determining the total time spent as inventory in days at different stages and the time spent in transit. For a particular SKU, based on past data, if the average times spent as inventory at the factory, warehouse, and area sales office are 4.2, 2.7, and 1.8 weeks, respectively, and if the average transit times for factory-warehouse and warehouse-area sales office are 0.8 and 0.5 weeks, respectively, then the supply chain from factory to area sales office is equal to $(4.2 + 2.7 + 1.8 + 0.8 + 0.5)$ weeks or 10 weeks. The variance (expectation of the squared deviation of a variable from its mean) in time taken at each stage enables us to statistically determine the variance of the total lead time and, hence, the probabilistic distribution of the total lead time. In the same example, if the variances in time spent as inventory at factory, warehouse, and area sales office are 6.0, 3.2, and 2.8 weeks-squared, respectively, and if the variances in transit times in factory-warehouse and warehouse-area sales office are 2.2 and 1.8 weeks-squared, respectively, then the supply chain variance from factory to area sales office is equal to $(6.0 + 3.2 + 2.8 + 2.2 + 1.8)$ weeks-squared or 16 weeks-squared. This calculation, of course, assumes that the variance at each stage is independent of the variance in other stages. Suitable modifications would need to be carried out if this assumption does not hold true. A variance of 16 weeks-squared implies a total lead-time standard-deviation of 4 weeks. If we assume the lead time to follow a normal distribution, we can then conclude that there is a 68.3% probability that the lead time is between 6 weeks (−1 standard deviation from mean lead time) and 14 weeks (+1 standard deviation from mean lead time), a 15.9% probability that the lead time is greater than 14 weeks, a 10% probability that the lead time is greater than 15.12 weeks (+1.28 standard deviation from mean lead time), and so on.

A thorough lead-time analysis would enable a firm to identify the supply chain stages that should be targeted for lead-time reduction (based on average lead-time statistics) and the supply chain stages that should be targeted for improving lead-time reliability (based on lead-time variance statistics). Thus, lead-time analytics is a strong pre-requirement for effective design of supply chain strategies for any firm where long and unreliable lead times are a matter of concern.

Supply chain cost-benefit analytics

Cost-benefit analysis is often carried out based only on the most expected scenarios. This results in decisions being taken with only the average level of a variable being the input. The variation in the variable value does not get captured if this approach is followed. An example of this is when a firm is evaluating two suppliers, effective cost of supplier one is reliable with a higher average (say $20–$22 per unit with an average of $21 per unit) while the effective cost of supplier two is unreliable with a lower average (say $17–$23 per unit with an average of $20 unit). Just considering the averages will prompt a firm to select supplier two while considering the variance would make supplier one more attractive. In many cost-benefit analyses, firms fail to include the effects of uncertainty. An example of this is about the right decision that should be taken in the example described in Table 4.1. The best scenario for the firm is when it orders only the minimum demand (demand that is definitely expected to happen) in January and orders the remaining demand after receiving the accurate estimate in late March. If the minimum demand for April is 500 units and if the unit cost of accurate procurement in late March is £640, then the firm orders 500 units in January at £560 and 500 units in late March at £640. The revenue on 1000 units would be £700,000, and the total procurement cost would be £600,000, resulting in a net profit of £100,000, which is higher than what we observed it would be had the procurement been through only one order in either January, February, or March.

How often do firms conduct supply chain cost-benefit analyses factoring uncertainties? The challenge is mainly in estimating uncertainty. We strongly argue that a deterministic supply chain cost-benefit analysis would be inferior to an analysis that factors in various uncertainties faced by the supply chain.

Strategic insights

• Excellent firms focus on analytics from an organizational perspective rather than with a piece-wise approach. Supply chain analytics is playing a significant role in the pursuit of supply chain excellence.

- Data analytics that study and analyze various uncertainties in the supply chain provide strategic insights to better design and manage supply chains.

Note

1 Bowers, M. R., Petrie, A., & Holcomb, M. C. 2017. Unleashing the potential of supply chain analytics. *MIT Sloan Management Review*, 59(1), 14.

11 Operations and supply chain management in the digital era

Contributed by Prasad Ramakrishnan
and Axel Zeijen

Prasad Ramakrishnan is a transformational global leader and change agent. He has lived and worked in North and South America, Europe, and Asia and has expertise in manufacturing and supply chain and product development across industries and countries. He led large, cross-functional, global teams in operations and strategy development and execution at Ford, Triumph, Alstom, and GE. He is skilled in senior-level negotiation, innovation, disruptive change management, and people development across cultures. He teaches in the graduate programs of universities in Boston and Zurich and is a board member and mentor in start-up ventures in the USA and Switzerland. He can be contacted at ramakrishnanprasad2@gmail.com.

Axel Zeijen is a doctoral student in Technology and Innovation Management at the Department of Management, Technology, and Economics at ETH Zurich in Switzerland. His research explores strategic management of technology and innovation. In this context, Axel studies the implications of new technologies on industries and organizations. He is interested in understanding how companies learn about, and respond to, new technologies at times of industrial transformations. Specifically, Axel's work focuses on transformative technologies, such as additive manufacturing, which require new ways for companies to deliver value, organize their supply chains, and manage their innovation projects. He can be contacted at azeijen@ethz.ch.

Unconventional solutions for unprecedented challenges

General Electric's Aviation division had a challenge. CFM International, its joint venture with Safran Aircraft Engines, was developing the new LEAP next generation commercial jet engine for better fuel efficiency and fewer emissions. Key success enablers included complex geometries of more than a dozen fuel passages inside the tip of the fuel nozzle, a critical component to spray fuel into the jet engine's combustor and mix with air in the most efficient manner. While the new design would deliver the performance needed, the failure of successive casting attempts made it appear impossible to manufacture by traditional methods. Additive manufacturing was a possibility but had only been used for prototypes, not for high-volume production. The team's subsequent success in solving this challenge enabled the launch of a successful commercial jet engine and a new division with unprecedented replication opportunities across the global company.

The team worked to re-engineer off-the-shelf 3-D printers and, instead of 20 individual parts that had to be welded and brazed together, used additive manufacturing to manufacture the new tip as a single piece with 25% less weight, five times more durability, and 30% more cost-efficiency. The next challenge was to scale up for mass production under a tight program schedule within stringent Federal Aviation Administration certification requirements. "People think 3D printing is as simple as operating an ink printer, but it's not," said Chris Schuppe[1] from GE Additive's AddWorks team, dedicated to accelerating additive adoption for GE's customers. "The fuel nozzle requires orchestrating over 3,000 layers of powdered metal that are about the thickness of a human hair."

GE brought together a multi-disciplinary team to resolve these challenges and, in 2015, built a new 3-D printing plant in Auburn, Alabama (USA), with over 40 3-D printers. From over 8,000 fuel nozzles in 2017, the plant had delivered over 33,000 3-D-printed fuel nozzles by late 2018 for use in engines like the Airbus A320neo jets, with orders valued at more than $236 billion.[2] GE's strong long-term commitment was evident in its acquiring an over $1 billion controlling investment in Sweden's Arcam AB, which uses electron beam printing, and Germany's Concept Laser, whose laser machines shape components from metallic powder.

Digital disruption in a VUCA world

3-D printing complex, dense parts like the fuel nozzle, with a fraction of the waste produced by conventional manufacturing, is an example of disruptive new technology breaking out of the prototype stage into a credible, monetizable manufacturing process. Welcome to digital disruption in a volatile, uncertain, complex, and ambiguous (VUCA) world. These disruptions entail challenges such as learning about the nature of new technologies, understanding application implications, and leading disruptive change that individuals and organizations need to meet.

What is new about the current wave of digital disruptions? In his book *The Fourth Age*,[3] Byron Reese suggests that technology fundamentally reshaped humanity three times in history before the current leaps in artificial intelligence and robotics. In addition, Steve Case[4] summarizes the leap of connectivity starting with the Internet, the rise of mobile app usage, and the Internet of Everything driving dramatic change across industries. Each wave of change in technology enabled successive productivity improvements leading to market disruption and further enhancements. Today, entry barriers have fallen with the steadily decreasing cost of software and hardware, sensors, storage, and bandwidth and the increase in predictive algorithms and machine-learning capabilities. The 1990s saw the emergence of foundations, such as industrial control and manufacturing and asset management software. The present generation of low-cost innovations enable companies to fully digitize operations – with a common *digital thread* through design, source, build, and service phases, using analytic intelligence to create a virtuous loop to deliver continuous improvements to customers.[5]

Digital manufacturing, industrial IoT (Internet of Things), and Industry 4.0 are all names that refer to this combined digital and physical transformation at the confluence of digital connectivity, advanced analytics, artificial intelligence, and new cyber-physical systems. Smart, connected products create unprecedented capabilities and functionality well beyond traditional product boundaries, disrupting and forcing a rethink of the entire value chain.[6] This offers a new set of choices about how value is created and monetized in an organization's business proposition, changing ecosystem partnerships and clarifying competitive advantages to be seized in the disruption. It goes beyond digitizing, making something electronic, to digitalizing – creating a business strategy around digitizing. Uber's successful disruption is an example, driving a shift in business proposition from owning a physical asset like a car to applying software and analytics to physical assets while offering new commercial relationships faster than the competition. Emerging developments, such as driver-less cars, further redefine abilities of smart, connected products (e.g., inter-connected Tesla vehicles) to function with complete autonomy, drastically reducing and redefining the human driver's role.

Amid this wave of digital disruption, there are initial attempts at building frameworks for responding to these changes. In this regard, Digital McKinsey explains that digital manufacturing could be actualized through levers to boost operational performance, defining new manufacturing strategies and designing the target digital manufacturing ecosystem.[7] In the future, the range of available software and hardware tools can enable responsive material tracking, augmented reality, collaborative robots, exoskeletons for increased load carrying, and emerging capabilities, such as machine learning and artificial intelligence. For example, asset performance management (or APM) is a combination of software and service offerings to help industrial and other asset-centric companies optimize the performance of their assets to increase availability, minimize costs, and reduce operational risks.

Such disruptions also require a major rethink of leadership, individual and team capability development across the organization, and investment in new technologies.

To what extent are organizations willing to invest in the ability for change in a VUCA world? According to a new IDC spending guide,[8] worldwide spending on Digital Transformation (DX) will be nearly $2 trillion by 2022. A big part of this spending would enable the transformation of global supply chains as companies and industries find ways to leapfrog customer-impacting productivity through innovative digital technology application. Complementary transformation in retail will include omni-channel commerce platforms, augmented virtual experience, in-store contextualized marketing, and next-generation payments.

The World Economic Forum's white paper[9] shares examples of investments in digital transformation made at the level of the production plant to enable manufacturing at the cutting edge of productivity with successful deployment at scale. In this context, Procter & Gamble's Rakona Plant in the Czech Republic provides a fine example, as the company drove productivity through digitalization to maintain the site's relevance despite shifting customer demands and increasing market pressure at P&G's second-oldest plant founded in 1875. In three years, the combined impact of these transformations resulted in reductions of customer complaints by 63%, inventory by 43%, off-quality products by 42%, changeover time by 36%, and full plant cost by 20% and in an overall productivity improvement of 160%.[8]

To fully understand the connection between emerging technologies and the new reality of supply chain management, it is imperative to dive one step deeper into a number of these technologies. Why and how are they applied, how do they affect supply chain management, and how can managers leverage their potential? The next sections provide short overviews of automation and cognitive technologies and artificial intelligence with a detailed look at additive manufacturing.

Cognitive technologies and artificial intelligence

Industries as varied as the textile and automotive industries have been using process automation for decades to achieve greater productivity, minimize human exposure to hazardous conditions, handle repetitive or difficult tasks, and seek efficiencies to reduce cost and support growth. Enhancements in sensor and vision technology have led to a change in this pattern, for example, with collaborative robots (or Cobots) that can work beside humans.[10] At the Ford Fiesta Plant in Cologne, Germany, for example, operators are working with Cobots to install shock absorbers on cars.[11] The Cobots, which are about three feet high and can stop immediately if sensors detect an arm in the path, lift and position shock absorbers into a wheel arch with humans completing the installation at the push of a button. This requires a rethinking of the role of people and the organization of processes in a plant, providing more opportunities for flexibility.

Collaborative Robots are an example of cognitive technologies,[12] defined as those technologies that can partially or totally take over tasks that have traditionally been performed by humans.[13] Industries are progressively increasing spending to deploy cognitive technologies in their products, processes, and services across various sectors.[14] Object identification and image classification are expected to be among the potential areas of opportunity for early implementation.[15] Beyond the projected $200 billion in cumulative direct spending on AI-specific hardware, software, and services are the larger economic benefits of cognitive technology deployments.

A related example of cognitive technology is software,[16] also called robotic process automation, that does repetitive tasks faster, more accurately, and more tirelessly than humans. This can free up humans to focus on strengths such as judgement and customer interface. Examples of tasks outsourced to RPA include invoice management at Siemens[17] using real-time ERP and workflow data, orchestrated by an integrated chatbot. Submission of insurance premium notes to a central repository at Xchanging,[18] a London stock-exchange-listed business process outsourcing company is another example. Selection of tasks to outsource, however, is critical while thoughtful deployment ensures that employees do not see automation as a threat to their jobs.

Artificial intelligence is emerging in many areas and is of special interest to companies undergoing digital disruption. In his book *The AI Advantage*,[19] Thomas H. Davenport describes three stages in the journey that companies can take toward achieving full utilization of artificial intelligence from *assisted intelligence*, to *augmented intelligence* and finally *autonomous intelligence*. A useful example of AI application along these three stages is cruise control automatically maintaining a vehicle's speed, lane detection systems using sensors to aid drivers, and self-driving cars operating with sensors and software. Another example is Deloitte Insights' description of artificial intelligence adoption at Google.[20]

The disruptive changes from cognitive technologies and artificial intelligence can affect the future of knowledge work similar to the impact of automation on the factory floor. They have the potential to replace work currently performed by humans with technology application through augmentation[21] – starting with what humans do today and figuring out how that work can be deepened rather than diminished by a greater use of machines.

Additive manufacturing

The current state of additive manufacturing

Given its great capacity to transform traditional manufacturing, it's important to go deeper into the type of digital disruption with which this chapter began. Additive manufacturing is the common name of a family of technologies which share the characteristics of building layers of materials additively (as opposed to subtracting) from digital models. This family of technologies has been in development since the mid-1980s, and new alternatives are being developed even today. Since the 2000s, some of the technologies have matured to the stage that they can produce parts whose quality is similar to or even higher than that of those made using traditional techniques. Technologies differ in the materials, usually polymers or metal. In his book *The Pan-Industrial Revolution*,[22] Richard D'Aveni outlines several technological principles employed.

AM is a powerful and versatile technology which strongly exhibits the uncertainty, complexity, and ambiguity represented by the VUCA world. A McKinsey survey found a lack of awareness of AM's applications and potential value.[23] Additionally, it highlighted that even with such awareness, organizational challenges are a further unsolved bottleneck. What are some important applications and implications?

Different dimensions of AM applications

A first distinction for AM applications in companies is the product manufactured – for what will 3-D printed parts eventually be used? Companies can additively manufacture prototypes, either for communicating ideas or functional testing. In this scenario, end-products would still be manufactured with traditional manufacturing techniques. Companies can also produce tools, moulds, or fixtures to aid in the manufacturing process. Finally, AM can also manufacture end-parts – both original products and spare parts – directly.

A second distinction is where AM is employed in the production process. AM can be used to enhance the R&D process. By giving physical shape to ideas, design engineers can be more effective and efficient in developing product designs. Companies can use AM to bridge lead times or resolve problems in supply chains. By quickly manufacturing a part that lasts until a replacement is delivered, costly downtime can be avoided. Finally, companies can use AM to produce spare parts. In some cases, this can even be done retroactively, by creating digital libraries of parts to replace valuable warehouse space.

A third distinction is in how value is pursued by using AM. This is highly dependent on the industry in which companies are operating. AM can save considerable time in going through product introduction processes by increasing both the speed of development (e.g., by quickly producing prototypes) and the breadth of search (e.g., by producing multiple variants of a part simultaneously). Industry-specific drivers of performance, such as strength, size and shape, or weight, can also favour AM. In aerospace applications, for example, AM can help save weight when redesigning parts using less material.

Several factors can be considered in identifying additive candidates, such as system complexity (multiple piece assembly or complex geometry), cost opportunity (multiple piece assembly, not a replacement for one-piece casting), durability challenges (machine tools limiting geometry, stress/thermals not optimized), and current size restrictions (equipment continuously increasing in size, complex geometry). Good additive geometries include those that cannot be manufactured using traditional methods (internal passages, lattice structures); prototype, low-volume, complex geometries; or those made from valuable materials normally requiring expensive moulds or tooling. Geometries designed for topology optimization to reduce weight or amount of material are also good candidates. Geometries not ideal for AM include those that can be easily turned on a lathe or mill or easily stamped, formed, or shaped. Additively producing a current design without redesign for AM will not unlock the technology's value.

Implications of additive manufacturing

Like the applications of AM, the implications of the technology can also be identified on different dimensions. A first distinction is how it affects the drivers of cost or value compared to traditional manufacturing technologies. Traditional techniques favour standardization and scale, but additive manufacturing follows different cost patterns. Rather than high investment and setup (fixed) costs with low variable costs, AM has low fixed costs but relatively high variable costs, favouring economies of scope to economies of scale. In traditional manufacturing, designs are kept as simple as possible to aid manufacturing processes. With AM, in contrast, complexity does not much hinder the production process and thus often comes free. This entails a shift from "design for manufacturing" to "design for value." Together, these two trends give rise to the possibility of "mass customization," where in theory every single part can be customized to customers' needs.

A second distinction is how AM affects the company and positioning in supply chains and industries. First, AM may affect companies' business models. If parts are printed, one can imagine that companies no longer seek to invest in manufacturing capabilities but rather outsource manufacturing to suppliers or even let customers print designs. AM can also affect the company setup since it is a technology that spans design and manufacturing. Keeping them separate will likely challenge the search for new solutions but bringing them together should be done carefully.

A third impact is the possibility of AM giving rise to new supply chain structures and intermediary layers. Already, we see companies specializing in supplying additively manufactured parts and advice to customers. A further example of this impact is the semiconductor industry, where integrated companies coexist with specialists that either design chips or manage the manufacturing facilities to produce them. This could be a future scenario for many industries employing AM. Higher-order effects may arise later in time but need consideration as well; if fixed costs of manufacturing drop, this will lower barriers to entry in many industries. Further, as AM becomes more widespread, we may expect future generations of products to be more accommodative to customization and upgradeability.

Finally, AM will likely affect critical capabilities in industries, and companies' added value in supply chains will depend on how well they can adapt. First, as design for additive manufacturing starts to take shape, this will challenge design engineers. Future designs will bring together technical disciplines and require new material science to inform the limits of designs. Companies can either choose to develop these design capabilities themselves or source them externally. Intellectual property in designs is another important area. As designs go digital, companies should think about new ways to protect their designs from copying or even reverse engineering with 3-D scanners. Finally, control over product design will become a key bottleneck in supply chains. AM works best when parts, and their distribution over value chains, are re-designed. This means that companies must think about, and leverage, technological designs and supply chain designs at the same time.

Additive manufacturing and 3-D printers can be considered new machine tools in manufacturing company toolkits. Mastering additive technologies would provide these companies with the ability to cover more applications and search for value in new ways while not directly replacing any other tools in companies' toolboxes. That said, additive manufacturing is not like any machine tool given its roots at the intersection of the digital and physical worlds and its main implications in how companies think about their designs and the shape of their value chains.

Additive manufacturing is a tool that cuts across many domains and requires new ways of thinking about design, value, and sourcing. Getting the strategy right in all these domains at the same time will be a game changer requiring nimble paradigm shifts in leadership thinking.

Leadership amidst disruptive change

Much has been written about the role of the leader combining strategic thinking with tactical delivery while engaging and developing employees including him- or herself. More than ever before, CEOs today consider attracting, retaining, and developing "next gen" leaders as a critical organizational priority. In this context, future supply chain leaders must have a clear and contemporary understanding of the new skills and capabilities required of future employees including technical, leadership, and higher cognitive skills. The focus of this section is to provide ways for a supply chain leader to stay current and lead amidst disruptive change. It assumes the leader has a strong foundation of successful delivery of objectives and is seeking to differentiate beyond basic expectations. Faced with unprecedented change in political, economic, social, technological, and future of work dimensions, the following five steps are a framework to chart a path of excellence.

First, it is more critical than ever for a supply chain leader to **understand the core value proposition of the organization**, the vital metrics indicating the organization's health measured against its mission, and quantitative and qualitative definitions of enterprise success. This understanding starts with the overall organization objectives but continues with crystal-clear traceability to supply chain fundamentals, simplifying and defining for themselves and their teams how the supply chain is a competitive advantage for the enterprise.

Second, supply chain leaders must develop practical and agile methods to **stay informed about relevant, current, and future general knowledge**. This includes horizon scanning (e.g., changing customer preferences, emerging technology disruptions, the impact of trade conditions such as tariffs and political upheavals on existing supply chain footprints), dialog and understanding of how competitors and other industries are pivoting their business models and practices in response, and connecting these data points back to evolving expectations of future directions within one's own organization.

Third, supply chain leaders must **reflect upon, and translate, knowledge into relevant strategic and tactical actions** with a holistic end-to-end view of their enterprise. For example, implementing 3-D printing may be an exciting manufacturing breakthrough but will necessitate the engagement of other impacted stakeholders with the need for different approaches to product design and the value chain to supply different raw materials and equipment. Political changes, such as tariffs, or socio-economic changes, such as rising wages, may make changing the global footprint look attractive but would require careful multi-scenario understanding and balancing of short- and long-term needs. It is the job of supply chain leaders to make the time to methodically and collaboratively step away from the daily delivery of existing commitments to evolve future strategy and tactics.

Fourth, **co-create social, environmental, and economic value in a sustainable way.**[24] *Live one's fundamental values* such as never compromising integrity and holding everyone to uniform high, principle-centred standards.[25] *Create practical ways to experiment and implement ideas* that impact the community – for example, ensuring wages and benefits protect both living standards and future security for employees and their families. *Seize social challenges as opportunities for practical co-creation* – for example ensuring gender equality in talent development and compensation. *Incorporate "cradle to cradle" vs. "cradle to grave" thinking*, not only in redefining the useful life and recyclability[26] of products and services but also in human dimensions, such as how to ethically and responsibly downsize a business.

The final step would be to **develop and maintain a personal leadership point of view (POV)** that enables one to learn, unlearn, and relearn to stay current and relevant as an effective leader to achieve operational success while being an inspiration to others. There are six actions supply chain leaders can take to enhance their POV. *Do something new* every month, and go beyond the expectations of your current role. *Take the risk of connecting* with people not normally in the circle of contacts – grow an active, virtual network covering different dimensions of functional, leadership, and aspirational subjects. *Actively shape the mission* of the organization by connecting one's role to objectives of higher levels of the organization, and find ways to leverage and operationalize this perspective. Identify one's own unique contribution – *what makes you special* – and build it into the way you lead, work, and live. *Be a force multiplier* by enabling individuals and teams to rise above the possible and exceed their own expectations. Finally, use every meeting or presentation opportunity to *tell a story* that goes beyond the content of presentation materials and captivates the imagination and emotions of the listeners.

Supply chain practices have evolved over decades as described throughout this book, with disruptive technology offering the promise of unprecedented productivity and future transformation of industries. However, the way forward is far from clear. Fundamental concepts like inventory management are undergoing dramatic paradigm shifts. For example, Wayfair, an e-commerce retailer, started as a one-stop online shopping experience for home décor products for the mass market without inventory or big-box outlet stores. Recently,[27] the opening of a store in Kentucky, USA, necessitates a change in their inventory strategy.

The supply chain leader of the future faces the exciting prospect of having new solutions through digitalization, cognitive technologies, additive manufacturing, and artificial intelligence to dramatically extend the realm of the possible. A new kind of supply chain beckons, with great opportunities to be inspiring and flexible in helping individuals, teams, and organizations to be effective at the intersection of technology and the future of work.

Notes

1 Electronic Component News. November 2018. *How a Walnut Sized Part Changed the Way GE Builds Jet Engines.* GE Reports.
2 GE Additive. October 2018. *New Manufacturing Milestone: 30,000 Additive Fuel Nozzles.* www.ge.com/additive/blog/new-manufacturing-milestone-30000-additive-fuel-nozzles
3 Reese, B. 2018. *The Fourth Age: Smart Robots, Conscious Computers, and the Future of Humanity.* Simon and Schuster.
4 Case, S. 2017. *The Third Wave: An Entrepreneur's Vision of the Future.* Simon and Schuster.
5 *GE's Digital Industrial Transformation Playbook.* www.ge.com/uk/sites/www.ge.com.uk/files/ge-digital-industrial-transformation-playbook-whitepaper.pdf
6 Porter, M. E., & Heppelmann, J. E. 2014. How smart, connected products are transforming competition. *Harvard Business Review*, 92(11), 64–88.
7 *Digital Manufacturing: Capturing Sustainable Impact at Scale.* www.mckinsey.it/file/7514/download?Token =CPK_xTY9
8 Independent Data Corporation. November 2018. *IDC Worldwide Semi-Annual Digital Transformation Spending Guide.*
9 *Fourth Industrial Revolution: Beacons of Technology and Innovation in Manufacturing.* www.weforum.org/whitepapers/fourth-industrial-revolution-beacons-of-technology-and-innovation-in-manufacturing
10 Marr, B. 2018. *The Future of Work: Are You Ready for Smart Cobots?* www.forbes.com/sites/bernardmarr/2018/08/29/the-future-of-work-are-you-ready-for-smart-cobots
11 Dignan, L. 2016. *Ford Tests Collaborative Robots in German Ford Fiesta Plant.* www.zdnet.com/article/ford-tests-collaborative-robots-in-german-ford-fiesta-plant/
12 *Cognitive Technologies: A Technical Primer.* https://www2.deloitte.com/insights/us/en/focus/cognitive-technologies/technical-primer.html
13 Schatsky D., Muraskin C., & Gurumurthy R., 2015. *Cognitive Technologies: The Real Opportunities for Business.* https://www2.deloitte.com/insights/us/en/deloitte-review/issue-16/cognitive-technologies-business-applications.html
14 *Worldwide Spending on Cognitive and Artificial Intelligence Systems Will Grow to $19.1 Billion in 2018.* https://www.idc.com/getdoc.jsp?containerId=prUS43662418
15 *Artificial Intelligence Use Cases.* www.tractica.com/research/artificial-intelligence-use-cases/
16 Lhuer, X. 2016. *The Next Acronym You need to Know About: RPA (Robotic Process Automation).* www.mckinsey.com/business-functions/digital-mckinsey/our-insights/the-next-acronym-you-need-to-know-about-rpa

17 *How Siemens Leverages Cognitive Technologies to Drive RPA Innovation.* www.blueprism.com/resources/case-studies/how-siemens-leverages-cognitive-technologies-to-drive-rpa-innovation
18 Willcocks, L. P., Lacity, M., & Craig, A. 2015. *Robotic Process Automation at Xchanging.* The Outsourcing Unit Working Research Paper Series (15/03). The London School of Economics and Political Science, London, UK.
19 Davenport, T. H. 2018. *The AI Advantage: How to Put the Artificial Intelligence Revolution to Work.* Cambridge, MA: MIT Press.
20 Mittal, N., Kuder, D., & Hans, S. 2019. *AI-fueled Organizations.* https://www2.deloitte.com/insights/us/en/focus/tech-trends/2019/driving-ai-potential-organizations.html
21 Davenport, T. H., & Kirby, J. 2015. Beyond automation. *Harvard Business Review*, 93(6), 58–65.
22 D'Aveni, R. 2018. *The Pan-Industrial Revolution: How New Manufacturing Titans Will Transform the World.* Houghton Mifflin.
23 Cohen, D. L. 2014. Fostering mainstream adoption of industrial 3D printing: Understanding the benefits and promoting organizational readiness. *3D Printing and Additive Manufacturing*, 1(2), 62–69.
24 Greenberg, D., McKone-Sweet, K., & Wilson, H. J. 2011. *The New Entrepreneurial Leader: Developing Leaders Who Shape Social and Economic Opportunity.* Berrett-Koehler Publishers.
25 Nair, K. 1994. *A Higher Standard of Leadership: Lessons from the Life of Gandhi.* Berrett-Koehler Publishers.
26 *What Is a Circular Economy? A Framework for an Economy that Is Restorative and Regenerative by Design.* www.ellenmacarthurfoundation.org/circular-economy/concept
27 Bhattacharyya, S. 2019. *Wayfair to Open Outlet Store to Recoup Costs from Excess Inventory.* https://digiday.com/retail/wayfair-open-outlet-store-recoup-costs-excess-inventory/

Brands, organizations, people, and places

Index